编辑说明

  根据第 24 届国际法哲学与社会哲学大会组委会的安排，本论丛主编与国际法哲学与社会哲学协会（IVR）司库、英国爱丁堡大学法学院教授 Zenon Bankowski 先生一道，从提交给第 24 届国际法哲学与社会哲学大会的论文中，选编了这本英文文集，作为论丛第十六辑，与在国内外另行出版的三本会议文集一道，构成了此次 IVR 北京大会正式刊行的文字性成果。

  本文集的作者为海外学者和我国港澳台地区学者，而在即将作为 IVR 会刊——《法哲学和社会哲学文汇》的增刊出版的另一大会英文文集的作者中，有数位来自中国大陆，这一刻意安排，旨在增进中外法哲学同仁的相互了解。

  本文集的选编还幸得国际法哲学与社会哲学协会秘书长 Claudio Michelon 先生的鼎力支持，谨此对他致以诚挚的感谢！同样的感谢还要送给为编者提供诸多便利的中国法学会和第 24 届国际法哲学与社会哲学大会的工作人员杨贝小姐、田力男女士、赵洪芳女士和朱明哲先生。

《法哲学与法社会学论丛》编委会
2011 年 3 年 11 日

Editor's Foreword

As arranged by the committee of XXIV World Congress of Philosophy of Law and Social Philosophy, the editor-in-chief of this Journal, together with the treasurer of International Association for Philosophy of Law and Social Philosophy (IVR), Professor Zenon Bankowski of Law School of University of Edinburg, UK, compiled this English anthology of selected essays from XXIV World Congress of IVR. The anthology has been edited into the 16th volume of the Journal which contributes to literal products formally published by IVR Beijing Congress with the other three separately published congress journals in and out of China.

The authors of this anthology are overseas scholars and Chinese scholars from Hong Kong and Taiwan, while some authors from mainland of China will present on the other English anthology coming soon as the supplement of *Archives for Philosophy of Law and Social Philosophy* (IVR's journal). This arrangement intends to enhance mutual understanding between Chinese scholars and foreign scholars of philosophy of law.

We owe much gratitude to Claudio Michelon, the Secretary-Genenal of IVR, for his support with the edition of this anthology. We are equally gratefully to China Law Society for its support as well as Miss Yang Bei, Ms. Tian Linan, Ms. Zhao Hongfang and Mr. Zhu Mingzhe for their efforts in the 24th IVR World Congress.

Editorial Committee of *Archives for Legal Philosophy and Sociology of Law*

目　录

〔美〕奥弗·拉班　法律确定性的谬误：为什么模糊的法律标准也许
　　更适合资本主义和自由主义？ …………………………………………… 1
〔西班牙〕迪亚哥·普尔　自由、价值和实践理性：奥卡姆与圣托马斯之
　　差异的当代相关性 …………………………………………………… 21
〔巴西〕努诺·科尔霍　亚里士多德论衡平和实践智慧：没有止境的
　　正义使命 ……………………………………………………………… 28
〔芬〕汉讷·伊索拉-米提伦　权衡与正当性：对法律原则权衡的反思 …… 36
〔斯洛文尼亚〕马里扬·帕夫克比克　〔奥〕弗里德里希·拉赫梅尔
　　论比例原则 …………………………………………………………… 60
〔意〕阿尔贝特·维斯帕兹阿尼　迈向一种对法律隐喻的诠释学路径 …… 69
〔土〕埃伊莱姆·尤米特·艾迪甘　衡平法在土耳其法司法裁量中的
　　角色及土耳其法官的衡平法观念 ……………………………………… 90
张嘉尹　法律的教义知识和跨学科研究：一个方法论的反思 …………… 107
黄维幸　法律方法论和科学哲学的契合：融合事实和法律 ……………… 126
〔巴西〕霍奥·查维斯　米歇尔·福柯的治理概念：对法律的最终否定 …… 154

本辑作者名录 …………………………………………………………… 167
引证体例 ………………………………………………………………… 169

CONTENTS

Ofer Raban The Fallacy of Legal Certainty: Why Vague Legal Standards May Be Better for Capitalism and Liberalism ·· 1

Diego Poole Freedom, Virtue and Practical Reason: the Present Relevance of the Differences between Ockham and St. Thomas ················· 21

Nuno M. M. S. Coelho Aristotle on Equity and Practical Wisdom: the Endless Task of Justice ·· 28

Hannele Isola-Miettinen Balancing and Legitimacy: the Reflections on the Balancing the Legal Principles ··· 36

Marijan Pavčnik Friedrich Lachmayer The Principle of Proportionality ··· 60

Alberto Vespaziani Towards a Hermeneutical Approach to Legal Metaphor ·· 69

Eylem Ümit Atilgan The Role of Equity in Judicial Discretion in Turkish Law and the Perception of Equity of Turkish Judges ················· 90

Chia-yin Chang Doctrinal Knowledge and Interdisciplinary Studies of Law: A Reflection on Methodology ··· 107

Thomas Weishing Huang Convergence of Legal Methodology and Philosophy of Science: The Fusion of Fact and Law ························· 126

João Chaves The Concept of Governmentality in Michel Foucault as His Last Negation of Law ··· 154

List of the Authors ·· 167
Citation Rules ·· 169

The Fallacy of Legal Certainty: Why Vague Legal Standards May Be Better for Capitalism and Liberalism*

Ofer Raban

Much has been written on the distinction between legal rules and legal standards: between bright-line rules framed in clear and determinate language, and vague standards employing indeterminate terms (like "reasonableness", "negligence", "fairness", or "good faith"). It is generally believed that rules provide the virtues of certainty and predictability, while standards afford flexibility, accommodate equitable solutions, and allow for a more informed development of the law.[1] This article seeks to refute the idea that bright-line rules are superior to vague standards in regard to certainty and predictability.

---

* I would like to thank Oliver Beige, Carl Bjerre, William Edmundson, Eric Ghosh, Dan Kahan, Jim Mooney, and Wojciech Zaluski for their helpful comments. The article will appear in the Boston University Public Interest Law Journal.

[1] See, e.g., fn. 2—7.

As we shall soon see, the refutation is so straightforward, and so obviously true, that one may be tempted to doubt whether any serious thinker claims otherwise. To allay this concern, here are a few prominent examples:

"Since the law should strive to balance certainty and reliability against flexibility, it is on the whole wise legal policy to use rules as much as possible for regulating human behavior because they are more certain than [standards]..." Joseph Raz, Legal Principles and the Limits of Law.[2]

"[S]tandards... increase the cost and difficulty of prediction [while] rules are defined [by] the ease with which private parties can predict how the law will apply to their conduct..." Louis Kaplow, The General Characteristics of Rules.[3]

"[T]he rule of law... implies (as the name suggests) a preference for rules over standards. Although a legislature, by issuing a standard, announces in advance of the regulated conduct that anyone who engages in that conduct now risks a sanction, in practice this announcement does not amount to much [because it] does not tell people what is permitted and what is not permitted, though it gives them something of an idea." Eric A. Posner, Standards, Rules, and Social Norms.[4]

"[A]nother obvious advantage of establishing as soon as possible [clear and definite rules]: predictability. Even in simpler times uncertainty has been regarded as incompatible with the Rule of Law. Rudimentary justice requires that those subject to the law must have the means of knowing what it prescribes." Antonin Scalia, The Rule of Law as a Law of Rules.[5]

"Since following a rule may produce a suboptimal decision in some particular case, the question of the comparative value of rule-based reliance is the question of the extent to which a decision-making environment is willing to tolerate suboptimal results in order that those affected by the decisions in that environment will be able to plan..." Frederick

---

[2] 81 *Yale L. J.* p. 823, pp. 841—842 (1972).
[3] *Encyclopedia of Law and Economics* (1999).
[4] 21 *Harv. J. L. & Pub. Pol'y*, p. 101, p. 113 (1997).
[5] 56 *U. Chi. L. Rev.* p. 1175, p. 1179, p. 1183 (1989).

Schauer, *Playing by The Rules*.[6]

"A system committed to the rule of law is...not committed to the unrealistic goal of making every decision according to judgments fully specified in advance. Nonetheless, ...[f]requently a lawmaker adopts rules because rules narrow or even eliminate the...uncertainty faced by people attempting to follow...the law. This step has enormous virtues in terms of promoting predictability and planning..." Cass R. Sunstein, Problems with Rules.[7]

These excerpts share the claim that bright-line rules allow people to predict the consequences of their actions better than vague legal standards. Thus, whenever a standard is chosen over an alternative rule, whatever the advantages otherwise gained, certainty and predictability suffer. This claim, to repeat, is mistaken.

I will examine this fallacy in the context of claims that clear legal rules produce the legal certainty and predictability required by capitalism and liberalism. As we shall soon see, the fallacy consists in identifying people's ability to predict the consequences of their actions with lawyers' ability to predict the consequences of applying the law. But the two can easily come apart: what may be perfectly certain and predictable for lawyers or judges applying the law may fly in the face of people's reasonable predictions. In fact, in many areas of the law clear rules are bound to produce less certainty and predictability than vague standards.

Section I articulates the claims that legal certainty and predictability are essential for capitalism and liberalism, and that these systems of economic and social organization therefore require legal rules framed in clear and determinate language. The first part of these claims is left unchallenged; but the assertion that certainty and predictability require bright-line rules is criticized in Section II, which argues that, oftentimes, the best-drafted clear and determinate rules would result in *less* certainty than alternative vague and indeterminate standards. Section IIII explains why things

---

[6] (Oxford University Press, 1991) p. 140. In an earlier paragraph Schauer notes that "the argument from reliance [i. e., predictability] ... presupposed a commonality of understanding between the relying addresses [i. e., those subjected to the law] and the enforcers [i. e., judges] on whose actins reliance is placed." That is absolutely correct, and is the reason why the best rules can reduce predictability when compared with vague standards. But instead of drawing the correct conclusion, Schauer moves to commit the fallacy by identifying rules with predictability insofar as addressees and enforcers' share "a common language". At p. 139. This is a typical mistake.

[7] 83 *Cal. L. Rev.*, p.953 (1995).

are so, arguing that the law is but one of many normative structures; that competing economic, social, or moral standards are often couched in vague and indeterminate terms; and that many of these standards cannot be reduced to clear and determinate rules. A short conclusion follows.

Ⅰ. Legal Certainty and Clear Legal Rules

We live in a capitalist liberal country, and these forms of economic and social organization obviously impose substantive conditions on the content of our laws: capitalism means that our laws must create and maintain a free and private economic sphere, while liberalism requires a zone of personal privacy free from private or public coercion. But some have claimed that capitalism and liberalism also impose some *formal* requirements on our laws: namely, that they be framed in clear and unambiguous language, and that they be applied in strict compliance with that language. The reason for these requirements, so goes the argument, is the importance of certainty and predictability for capitalism and liberalism.

Capitalism

The importance of legal certainty to capitalism was famously articulated in Max Weber's classic (posthumous) *Economy and Society*. "Capitalistic enterprise... cannot do without legal security", wrote Weber, because such security was essential for the investment of capital.[8] If an entrepreneur is to build a factory on a piece of land, she needs to be secure in her ownership of the land; she needs to know that the contracts she signs with the contractors are enforceable; she needs to know what taxes she will be asked to pay; in short, she needs to know where she stands vis-à-vis her expected costs and expected income. "[B]ourgeois interests", said Weber, need a legal system that "function[s] in a calculable way"; and calculability meant, in turn "an unambiguous and clear legal system".[9] An economy where private parties own, produce, exchange, and consume articles of

---

[8] Max Weber, *Economy and Society*, Guenther Roth & Claus Wittich eds., Univ. of California Press, 1978, p. 833.
[9] Ibid., p. 847.

value, free from public or private coercion, must provide private actors with a clear and certain delimitations of their economic rights and duties; and these delimitations necessitate clear and determinate legal rules. Indeed Weber believed that Western law's facilitation of capitalism was a function of the fact that it operates "like a slot machine into which one just drops facts... in order to have it spew out decisions".[10] As others have since elaborated this thesis, "markets cannot function without a clear and precise definition of who owns what (property rights), who may do what to whom (civil and criminal law), and who must pay whom to protect their interests (contract law)".[11] The idea that capitalism requires clear and determinate legal rules (as opposed to vague and indeterminate standards) is widely accepted today.

Liberalism

An analogous claim has been made about liberalism—namely, that clear and determinate legal rules are essential for freedom. Friedrich Hayek explained the thesis as follows: "The law tells what facts [the individual] may count on[,] and thereby extends the range within which he can predict the consequences of his actions."[12] "[T]he coercive acts of government become data on which the individual can base his own plans... so that in most instances the individual need never be coerced unless he has placed himself in a position where he knows he will be coerced."[13] Consequently, "freedom is dependent upon certain attributes of the law, its generality and certainty, and the restrictions it places on the discretion of authority".[14] "[A]ll coercive action of government must be unambiguously determined", proclaimed Hayek.[15] And he strongly condemned the use of vague legal standards like "reasonableness" or "fairness": "One could write a history of the decline of the rule of Law", he wrote, "in terms of the progressive introduction of these vague for-

---

[10] Ibid., p. 886.
[11] Daniel W. Bromley, *Economic Interests and Institutions: the Conceptual Basis of Public Policy*, 1989.
[12] Friedrich Hayek, *The Constitution of Liberty*, 1978, pp. 156—157.
[13] Ibid., p. 21.
[14] Ibid., p. 167.
[15] Ibid., p. 222.

mulas into legislation and jurisdiction, and of the increasing arbitrariness and uncertainty of... the law and the judicature".[16]

Let me exemplify Hayek's insight with a personal anecdote. A couple of years ago I participated in an academic conference in a European city I was keen to explore. Carefully examining the conference's program, I marked for myself those presentations I planned to attend, expecting to spend the hours between them sightseeing. Alas, the person responsible for keeping the schedule was an Italian national with the insouciant sense of time common to his people: sessions regularly began late, regularly ended late, and last-minute changes in the program were not uncommon. As per Hayek, this uncertainty ruined my ability to maximize my freedom. To give another analogy: if stones fall down from the sky in an unpredictable pattern, one's freedom of movement is seriously constrained; but if they fall down in a pre-determined pattern, one can avoid the times and places where they fall, and walk freely anytime and everywhere else. Clear and determinate legal rules allow people to know where they stand (and where they should not stand) and therefore allow them to maximize their freedom.

Legal Interpretation

One corollary of the claim that clear and determinate legal rules are essential for certainty and predictability pertains to the proper method of legal interpretation: unless courts faithfully follow such rules' clear and determinate language, so goes the argument, the certainty and predictability they are supposed to secure would be undermined. Thus advocates of the textualist method—the idea that judges should strictly follow the language of legal rules—believe that textualism's great virtue is that it allows people to better predict the consequences of their actions.[17]

---

[16] Hayek, *The Road to Serfdom*, 1944, p. 78.
[17] See, e. g. , Frank H. Easterbrook, "Text, History, and Structure in Statutory Interpretation", 17 *Harv. J. L. & Pub. Pol'y* p. 61, p. 63 (1994); "Textualism and the Equity of the Statute", 101 *Colum. L. Rev.* 1, p. 58 (2001).

II. The Fallacy of Legal Certainty

The claims that strictly construed clear and determinate legal rules are essential for capitalism and liberalism are intuitive and widespread. But they are based on a confusion between the predictability of applying a legal rule, and the predictability of that rule's results for those it governs. As we saw, capitalism and liberalism require the latter, not the former: what we want is a certain and predictable regulative environment (a predictable economic sphere, a predictable social sphere), not merely clear and determinate rules generating certain and predictable outcomes. And in fact, clear and determinate rules would often produce less predictable environments than vague legal standards. Here are some examples.

Capitalism

Contract law lies at the heart capitalism's legal framework, and disputes over the best contract doctrines often implicate issues of predictability. One such famous dispute concerns the admissibility of external evidence bearing on the interpretation of clear and unambiguous contractual provisions. According to the traditional rule, if a contractual provision is clear and unambiguous, no extrinsic evidence—like evidence of oral promises, implicit understandings, or industry practice—can be brought to support a different interpretation. This is a clear and unambiguous contracts rule that—say its advocates—provides contractual parties the certainty and predictability they need. But a minority of courts adopted a much vaguer standard, one that admits extrinsic evidence if "the offered evidence is relevant to prove a meaning to which the language of the instrument is reasonably susceptible".[18] Thus, even if a contractual provision appears perfectly clear, a party can introduce external evidence showing that the parties intended a different meaning if that meaning is a reasonable one.

For example, in the case referenced above the plaintiff entered into a contract to remove and replace the upper metal cover of the defendant's steam turbine. A contractual provision declared that the plaintiff agreed to indemnify the defendant "a-

---

[18] PG&E v. G. W. Thomas Draynage & Rigging Co., 69 Cal. 2d 33 (1968).

gainst all loss, damage, expense and liability resulting from... injury to property, arising out of or in any way connected with the performance of this contract". During the work, a piece of metal fell and damaged the turbine. The defendant claimed that the plaintiff had to indemnify for the damage; but the plaintiff offered to introduce extrinsic evidence showing that the indemnity clause was meant to cover only injury to the property of third parties, not plaintiff. The trial court adhered to the traditional rule and held that since the relevant contractual provision was clear and unambiguous, that was the end of the matter. But the California Supreme Court reversed: the Court replaced the traditional rule with the vaguer "extrinsic evidence" standard, and held that, under the new standard, the evidence should be admitted.[19]

Various commentators considered the decision a blow to the certainty needed by economic actors. As one commentator put it:

> The problem with using extrinsic evidence to establish that the plain meaning of a term in a contract is not, in fact, its meaning is that the use of the extrinsic evidence for such a purpose creates uncertainty. The primary basis of contract law is to provide certainty to the contracting parties. Court decisions eliminating this certainty do not aid [contractual parties]. Neither party can be sure that express, plain terms will be enforced. If either party can convince the fact-finder that the intent was something other than what the plain terms suggest, these plain terms will be ignored. This is the opposite of certainty.[20]

Many courts agree with this assessment—including, to name some of the more prominent ones, the 9th Circuit Court of Appeals, the Canadian Supreme Court, and

---

[19] Other courts soon followed suits. See, e.g., William Blair & Co. v. FI Liquidation Corp., 830 N. E. 2d 760,773—774 (Ill. App. Ct. 2004); Cafeteria Operators, L. P. v. Coronado-Santa Fe Assocs., L. P., 952 P. 2d 435,446 (N. M. Ct. App. 1997); Taylor v. State Farm Mut. Auto. Ins. Co., 854 P. 2d 1134, 1140—1141 (Ariz. 1993)(en banc); Denny's Rests., Inc. v. Sec. Union Title Ins. Co., 859 P. 2d 619,626 (Wash. Ct. App. 1993); Admiral Builders Sav. & Loan Assoc. v. South River Landing, Inc., 502 A. 2d 1096,1099 (Md. Ct. Spec. App. 1986); Alyeska Pipeline Serv. Co. v. O'Kelley, 645 P. 2d 767,771 n. 1 (Alaska 1982).

[20] David F. Tavella, "Are Insurance Policies Still Contracts?", 42 *Creighton L. Rev.* p. 157 (2009).

the English House of Lords.[21] While the traditional rule ("clear and unambiguous contractual provisions are enforced as written") allows parties to easily predict the consequences of their contractual provisions, the new standard—so goes the claim—introduces a great measure of uncertainty by making the meaning of contractual provisions depend on whether other "reasonable" interpretations can be demonstrated.

But in fact, and rather obviously so, the *very purpose* of the new standard is to accord with people's predictions and expectations. After all, if there really was an understanding between the parties that indemnification was due only in case of damage to third parties, the expectations of the parties would be frustrated by the traditional rule. But differently, people do not simply expect their contractual provisions to be enforced, they expect *their understandings of these provisions* to be enforced; and the introduction of external evidence allows them to prove such understandings in cases where these diverge from the contract's literal language. The traditional brightline rule allows more certainty and predictability *for the lawyers and judges who apply the law*, but not for the economic actors who engage in contractual transactions.

Faced with the obvious fact that the predictions of economic actors may be frustrated rather than enhanced by the traditional rule—and may be better-respected under the new and vaguer standard—the advocates of the traditional rule fall back on a related argument: they insist that although predictability may suffer in this particular case, *overall predictability* nonetheless improves when courts refuse to open up the meaning of clear and unambiguous provisions to challenges by other "reasonable" in-

---

[21] See *Travelers Ins. Co. v. Budget Rent-A-Car Systems, Inc.*, 901 F. 2d 765 (9th Cir. 1990) ("The rule... [allowing extrinsic evidence is] dangerous because it adds a heaping measure of uncertainty where certainty is essential. Insurance companies, like other commercial actors, need predictability; they write their contracts in precise language for that reason, and they calculate their premiums accordingly. When insurance contracts no longer mean what they say, it becomes exceedingly difficult to calculate risks. ... [W]e doubt that such a... [rule] serves the long-term interest of those whose livelihood depends upon certainty and predictability in the enforcement of commercial contracts."); *Shogun Finance v. Hudson*, [2004] A. C. 919, 944 (H. L.) (U. K.) ("This rule [barring extrinsic evidence in contract interpretation] is one of the great strengths of English commercial law and is one of the main reasons for the international success of English law in preference to laxer systems which do not provide the same certainty."). See also Stephen Waddams, "Modern Notions of Commercial Reality and Justice: Justice Iacobucci and Contract Law", 57 *U. Toronto L. J.* 331 (2007) ("Justice Iacobucci's emphasis on the merits of certainty in commercial transactions was reflected also in his rather strict formulation of the rule excluding extrinsic evidence in interpreting contracts, in a patent case decided five years later, *Eli Lilly & Co. v. Novopharm Ltd.*, [1998] 2 S. C. R. 129, 161 D. L. R. (4th) 1, where he wrote the unanimous judgment of the [Canadian Supreme] Court.").

terpretations. After all, allowing such challenges makes it more difficult to predict what a contractual provision might be read to mean, and thus reduces the ability of *most* contractual parties to predict the consequences of their contracts.

The claim has little to support it. First, this is an *empirical* claim, a claim whose accuracy cannot be derived from the thesis (indeed the truism) that the application of clear and unambiguous rules is more predictable than the application of vague standards. The claim asserts that, *as an empirical matter*, most economic actors would have a better shot at predicting the meaning of their contractual provisions if these were enforced literally and not allowed to be challenged by alternative "reasonable" interpretations. The veracity of this allegation depends, therefore, on answers to a number of empirical questions, including:

—How many contract disputes involve attempts to introduce extrinsic evidence in support of interpretations that were never in fact agreed to?

—How many of these attempts succeed?

—How many people in fact rely on oral promises or industry practices, so that a literal reading of their contracts may not accurately reflect their agreements?

—How many people can we expect to be aware of a legal rule that refuses to consider claims of oral promises or industry practices?

—What is the extent to which people can draft contracts whose literal texts accurately reflect their agreements (often in contexts they did not explicitly contemplate)?

These are some of the questions that those who claim that the traditional rule advances "overall predictability" never bother to ask, let alone answer; but the answers are essential for their claim. There can be no automatic transition from the predictability of a legal rule to the predictability we actually care about—that of contractual obligations. A legal rule that is perfectly certain and predictable to the lawyers and judges applying it may be perfectly harmful to the certainty and predictability required by capitalism.

In fact, the likelihood that the traditional rule *harms* overall certainty and predictability is substantial. Whether we consider external evidence or whether we blindly follow the literal text, we always stand the risk of frustrating the parties' predictions and expectations; but in the former case we at least consciously deliberate about our decision: we consciously seek to align the legal outcome with the parties' predictions. The traditional rule, by contrast, lets the vagaries of circumstance determine the outcome. In short, there is precious little to suggest that the traditional bright-line rule brings more certainty and predictability than its vaguer alternative.

Liberalism

Clear and determinate legal rules can also reduce our freedom. Take the crime of rape, defined in many American jurisdictions as "sexual intercourse accomplished with force and without consent".[22] Since the notions of "force" and "consent" are vague, determining whether rape occurred can be notoriously difficult: courts habitually face ambiguous situations involving passive victims and aggressive but non-violent defendants, where the presence of force or the absence of consent are difficult to determine. Such indeterminacy in the definition of a crime carrying long years of imprisonment seems to fly in the face of Hayek's insistence that "all coercive action of government must be unambiguously determined..." And so, unsurprisingly, the definition has been subjected to much criticism.[23]

Some of the critics of the present definition have been calling for its replacement with a clear and determinate rule. One such proposal involves the requirement of "explicit verbal consent": in the absence of explicit verbal consent to an intercourse, and assuming a complaining victim, rape had been committed.[24] There would be no need to undertake the thorny question of whether some form of *implicit* consent was given; instead, here is a clear and straightforward legal regime, one that gives potential victims and defendants a clearer notice as to where they stand, and which thereby allows them to maximize their freedom by avoiding placing themselves in legally ambiguous situations.

But in actual fact, such legal regime would only *increase* uncertainty. Remember that the certainty with which we are concerned pertains to the ability of actors to predict the consequences of their actions, *not* the ability of lawyers to predict the ap-

---

[22]　See, e.g., Kan. Stat. Ann. § 21-3502(a)(1)(A)(2008)(Kansas' rape statute).
[23]　Friedrich Hayek, *The Constitution of Liberty*, p. 222.
[24]　The proposal has even been implemented as campus policy in one American university: Antioch College in Ohio adopted a sexual offense policy that requires "willing and verbal" consent for each sexual touching. See Jane Gross, "Combating Rape on Campus In a Class on Sexual Consent", N. Y. Times, Sept. 25, 1993, http://query.nytimes.com/gst/fullpage.html?res=9F0CE1DB1239F936A1575AC0A965958260&fta=y.

plication of a legal rule. And while the rule mandating "explicit verbal consent" may be very predictable in application, it would make it very difficult to predict the legal consequences of one's actions. After all, given prevalent social norms, explicit verbal consent is unlikely in many cases of perfectly legitimate and consensual intercourse, whatever the law says on that matter. Thus, a definition of rape that regards a complaining victim, an intercourse, and the absence of verbal consent as sufficient for conviction would subject many such legitimate (and hence likely) actions to a forbidding criminal punishment whenever someone would be interested in filing a complaint. Once again, a clear and unambiguous rule whose application is perfectly predictable would produce a very risky and unpredictable social environment for actors looking to predict the consequences of their actions.

Legal Interpretation

It should be obvious by now that courts would often *reduce* certainty and predictability when they act as textualists and faithfully follow the clear language of bright-line rules. But, once again, courts often miss that point. Take, for example, *Devillers v. Auto Club Ins Assn.* (2005), a case decided by the Michigan Supreme Court, where self-proclaimed textualists hold a majority. The case applied a Michigan statute limiting claimants' ability to recover from insurance companies that improperly deny coverage. The statute read: "[A] claimant may not recover [insurance] benefits for any... loss incurred more than 1 year before the date on which the [legal] action was commenced."[25] This meant that a claimant who was *entitled* to collect insurance payments but was improperly denied coverage was nevertheless barred from recovering for any loss incurred a year or more before the date her lawsuit was filed. The statute, which functions as a statute-of-limitations for insurance claims, seeks to enforce speedy resolutions of denial-of-coverage disputes.

The case before the Michigan court involved a variation on the familiar theme: in *Devillers*, the insurance company corresponded with the insured for *two years* before finally denying his claim. Once the claim was denied the insured sued, but the court held for the insurance company, allowing recovery only for the one-year period before the lawsuit was filed (hence disallowing recovery for the costlier one year im-

---

[25] Mich. Comp. Laws § 500.3145 (2008).

mediately following the injury). The court rejected the claim that the period of recovery should have been tolled until the moment coverage was denied. The statutory language, said the opinion, was clear and unambiguous; and "if the words of the statute are clear, the actor should be able to expect, that is, rely, that they will be carried out by all in society, including the courts. In fact, should a court confound those legitimate citizen expectations by [failing to faithfully follow the text of the statute], it is that court itself that has disrupted the reliance interest".[26]

Here was the fallacy of legal certainty in its glorious folly: in the name of legal certainty and predictability, the Michigan Court required people to sue their insurance companies before they knew they had a reason to sue, or even to consult an attorney.[27] The court mistook the predictability of legal interpretation for the predictability of the consequences of one's actions. A textualist methodology may promote the former predictability, but not always the latter; and, once again, it is the latter that accounts for the importance of certainty and predictability in our law.

Indeed the Michigan court made its confusion even more explicit when, referring to a dissenting judge who deplored the opinion's textualist methodology, it responded: "What are the standards upon which litigants can reasonably predict his [i.e. the dissenter's] future interpretations, the rule of law being dependent upon such predictability?"[28] But litigants' (or, more accurately, people's) concern is, first and foremost, with predicting their rights and duties under their insurance policies, not the "future interpretations" of insurance law. And while sometimes they would use the latter to achieve the former, oftentimes (as here) they would not.

At this point in the argument it may be tempting to revert to the *overall predictability* claim: the claim that although the Michigan court may have frustrated reasonable expectations in this particular case, predictability is enhanced *overall* when courts consistently employ a textualist analysis. But that claim, once again, depends on a host of highly dubious empirical propositions that are simply assumed,

---

[26] Ibid., p. 585.

[27] This preposterous result was no isolated event: within a short time of declaring itself strict constructionist, that Michigan court made a number of decisions that would have surprised and appalled not only those subjected to them, but also the legislators whose policy choices it purported to implement. *See, e. g.*, Cameron v. Auto Club Ins. Ass'n, 476 Mich. 55 (2006); People v. Chavis, 486 Mich. 84 (2003).

[28] Ibid.

but never defended.[29]

One of those is the proposition that, *on the whole*, people base their predictions regarding the consequences of their actions on statutory texts. But most people who buy insurance, or sign contracts, or do whatever it is people do that lands them in legal disputes, are not likely to acquaint themselves with the dozens or hundreds of legal rules governing their action. Only when a problem arises do they examine (or consult someone who examines) the words of the governing statutes—by which time it is too late. Legal rules inhabit a world replete with non-legal norms that are often more influential than the law in shaping people's predictions and expectations. As John Austin once observed, legislators and lawyers tend to "forget that positive law may be superfluous or impotent, and therefore may lead to nothing but purely gratuitous vexation. They forget that the moral or religious [or economic or social or cultural] sentiment of the community" may dictate people's expectations far more than the law itself.[30]

Moreover, even willingness and ability to consult the law in advance, and to act accordingly, would be futile in many cases, since people often do not know which legal rule would end up governing their legal dispute. For instance, few people anticipate being subjected to the rules governing mutual mistake in contract formation, and so few could take those into account in contemplating their contracts. A textualist analysis—or, for that matter, clear and unambiguous rules—can facilitate predictability only when people can configure them into their predictions. But oftentimes that is not the case.

In short, there is little reason to think that courts engaged in textualist interpretation can better promote predictability. This is especially true given that only non-textualist interpretation (which often, of course, ends up following the text) can deliberately take into account people's expectations.

---

[29] See Section II above, the discussion of the "external evidence rule" under "capitalism".

[30] John Austin, *The Province of Jurisprudence Determined and the Uses of the Study of Jurisprudence*, Isaiah Berlin et al. eds., Weidenfeld and Nicholson, 1954 (1832), p. 162.

III. Why Vague Standards May Enhance Certainty

Vagueness and Certainty

Here is one last objection: it may indeed be the case that the "external evidence" rule or the "explicit verbal consent" rule may produce less certainty than their vaguer alternatives; but those who believe that clear and unambiguous rules produce more certainty and predictability than vague standards need not think that *any* clear rule does so. The claim pertains only to *well-crafted* rules, not to ill-conceived ones; and the "external evidence" rule, or the rule of "explicit verbal consent", may be simply ill-conceived. The proper comparison is therefore between well-crafted and strictly-followed clear and unambiguous rules and well-crafted vague standards: it is here that bright-line rules are bound to perform better predictability-wise.

A few responses are in order. First, a good many jurists consider the "external evidence" rule and the suggestion of "explicit verbal consent" perfectly well-conceived. Indeed these rules are not figments of my imagination: they are the real-life suggestions of those who seek better certainty and predictability in these areas of the law. More fundamentally, the objection assumes that there always is a clear and determinate bright-line alternative that would perform better, predictability-wise, than a vague standard. But what could support that assumption??? Indeed my argument is that in many areas of the law (including contracts or rape) bright-line rules would *never* produce more predictability than alternative nebulous standards. The problem with the "external evidence" rule or with "explicit verbal consent" is not that they are ill-conceived, but that they seek to reduce the irreducible.

Here is an example of what I mean by that. A number of states, as well as the federal government, have adopted statutes that penalize "unfair competition", understood as commercial practices that deceive consumers. These criminal statutes use highly vague and indeterminate phraseology in defining the illegal conduct. California's unfair competition law, for instance, criminalizes "unfair or fraudulent business act or practice and unfair, deceptive, untrue or misleading advertising..."[31] Defendants challenged the statute as unconstitutional because of its "uncertainty and vagueness", but a California court rejected the challenge by maintaining that California *could not* draft a more determinate statute: "it would be impossible to draft in advance detailed plans and specifications of all acts and conduct to be prohibited... since unfair or fraudulent business practices may run the gamut of human ingenuity and chicanery."[32] The court went on to cite a U.S. Supreme Court opinion, which (itself citing a congressional report) stated: "It is impossible to frame [clear and unambiguous] definitions which embrace all unfair practices. There is no limit to human inventiveness in this field. Even if all known unfair practices were specifically defined and prohibited, it would be at once necessary to begin over again. If Congress were to adopt the method of definition, it would undertake an endless task."[33] In fact, any alternative statute would substantially reduce the certainty and predictability that facilitate economic transactions: allowing consumer deception to go unpunished would make for a far more uncertain economic environment for both consumers and suppliers.

A similar impossibility with avoiding vagueness can be seen in the proposal of "explicit verbal consent" in the definition of rape. After all, people can be *coerced* to provide such consent. Thus, any regime of verbal consent must also include an inquiry as to whether the consent was voluntary—an inquiry that reintroduces (if at a different level) the very vagueness that the verbal consent regime sought to replace. And, obviously, a failure to include that vague inquiry is bound to confound everyone's expectations.

Multi-Dimensional Situations

Now why is that? Why is it that, in certain areas of the law, bright-line are *bound* to result in less certainty and less predictability that relatively vague and indeterminate standards? The short answer is that certain subject matters simply do not

---

[31] California's Unfair Competition Law, California Business & Professions Code § 17200.
[32] People v. Nat'l Research Co. of Cal., 201 Cal. App. 2d 765 (1962).
[33] Schecter Poultry Corp. v. U.S., 295 U.S. 495, 532, 55 S. Ct. 837, 844 (1935) (citing Fed. Trade Comm'n v. R. F. Keppel & Bro., 291 U.S. 304, 312, 54 S. Ct. 423, 426 (1934)).

lend themselves to reduction to clear and unambiguous rules. As Aristotle noted long ago, "precision is not to be sought for alike in all discussions..."[34] And "precision"—or, if you will, linguistic clarity and unambiguousness—is often lacking in descriptions of human mental states, which are (unsurprisingly) prevalent in both legal and non-legal norms (including the concepts of "coercion", "deception", "fairness", "reasonableness", "negligence", "recklessness", "good faith", "malice", "intention"—the list goes on and on). These concepts, and the phenomena they describe, are informed by various combinations of factors having different, and varying, imports. Determining whether a person was "negligent", or whether she was "coerced", resembles making a diagnosis under the Diagnostic and Statistical Manual of Mental Disorders of the American Psychiatric Association, where a disorder is said to exist whenever, say, eight of fifteen factors of varying importance and of varying possible combinations are present.[35] Such definitions seek to capture something of a pattern, a *gestalt*, a feature made up of various elements neither of which is necessary or sufficient, where the presence or absence of one element may impact the importance or weight of the others.

Lon Fuller, in a posthumously published article entitled *The Forms and Limits of Adjudication*, asked a question similar to the one I am asking here: "What tacit assumptions", asked Fuller, "underlie the conviction that certain problems are inherently unsuited for adjudicative disposition?"[36] Adjudication, for Fuller, consisted in the articulation of rules or principles "which can give meaning to the demand that like cases be given like treatment".[37] But certain resolutions do not lend themselves to that demand. The question, for Fuller, was "which?" When was it futile, or ineffective, to try to decide a case by articulating a governing rule? The question I am asking is similar: in what circumstances it is futile, or ineffective, to try to decide a case by articulating a clear and unambiguous rule rather than a vague standard? Fuller's question concerns a different point along the same continuum.

---

[34] Aristotle, *Nicomachean Ethics*, W. Ross trans. 1940, pp. 13—14.

[35] Indeterminate and vague legal standard can therefore presumably be reduced (though with considerable difficulty and possibility of error) into such multi-factor multi-weight legal tests; but such tests are as different from clear legal rules as the vague standards they would replace.

[36] 92 *Harv. L. Rev.* p. 353 (1978).

[37] Ibid., p. 368.

Fuller's answer appealed to the notion of "polycentric situations", borrowed from Michael Polanyi's *The Logic of Liberty* [38], which concern situations having multiple elements with mutual influence over each other:

> We may visualize this kind of situation by thinking of a spider web. A pull on one strand will distribute tensions after a complicated pattern throughout the web as a whole. Doubling the original pull will, in all likelihood, not simply double each of the resulting tensions but will rather create a different complicated pattern of tensions. ...This is a "polycentric" situation because it is "many centered"—each crossing of strands is a distinct center for distributing tensions.

Fuller gave a simple example:

> Suppose...it were decided to assign players on a football team to their positions by a process of adjudication. I assume that we would agree that this is...unwise... It is not merely a matter of eleven different men being possibly affected; each shift of any one player might have a different set of repercussions on the remaining players: putting Jones in as quarterback would have one set of carryover effects, putting him in as left end, another. Here, again, we are dealing with a situation of interacting points of influence and therefore with a polycentric problem beyond the proper limits of adjudication.

Likewise, such polycentric situations are best-governed by vague standards and not by clear rules.

Many of our social, moral, and economic decisions involve polycentric determinations; and why wouldn't they? Life can be complicated... And so it is unsurprising that our normative standards are replete with such concepts—and that, consequently, so are our laws, which are often mere formalizations of these non-legal (or pre-legal) standards. Thus, vague and indeterminate legal standards often produce more certainty and predictability than any alternative bright-line rule because they replicate, one-for-one, the social, moral, economic, or political norm that already prevails, and which, given the nature of the phenomenon it describes, can not be reduced to clear and unambiguous language.

---

[38] M. Polanyi, *The Logic of Liberty*: Reflections and Rejoinders, 1951, p.171.

IV. Conclusion

Capitalism and liberalism thrive when people can predict the consequences of their actions and can thereby maximize economic efficiency and personal freedom. But such predictability is distinct from the predictability of applying legal rules to given cases. Looking at the world with their professional bias, jurists often fail to distinguish between these two sorts of predictability (and so it should come as no surprise that both Max Weber and Friedrich Hayek were also lawyers). While clear and determinate legal rules are superior, *by definition*, insofar as the predictability of application is concerned, vague legal standards are often better in allowing people to predict the consequences of their actions.

Friedrich Hayek, for all his early insistence on "unambiguous rules fixed and announced beforehand", had come to realize this later in life.[39] In 1973, at age 74, he wrote:

> This [last remark] throws important light on a much discussed issue, the supposed greater certainty of the law under a system in which all rules of law have been laid down in written or codified form, and which the judge is restricted to applying such rules as have become written law. In my own case even the experience of thirty odd years in the common law world was not enough to correct this deeply rooted prejudice, and only my return to a civil law atmosphere has led me seriously to question it. Although legislation can certainly increase the certainty of the law on particular points, I am now persuaded that this advantage is more than offset if its recognition leads to the requirement that only what has thus been expressed in statutes should have the force of law. It seems to me that judicial decision may in fact be more predictable if the judge is also bound by generally held views of what is just, even when they are not supported by the letter of the law...[40]

One may wonder what, if anything, remains of Hayek's decades-long insistence on clear and determinate legal rules announced in advance and faithfully followed. But be that as it may, Hayek is certainly correct that a legal regime containing vague

---

[39] Hayek, *The Road to Serfdom*, p. 72.
[40] Friedrich Hayek, *Law, Legislation, and Liberty*, 1978, p. 117.

moral standards (indeed *unwritten* moral standards!) may often produce more certainty and predictability than strictly-construed clear and determinate rules.

Hayek's insight should receive wider recognition. It has long been recognized that vague legal standards and a non-textualist judiciary would often produce better regulative results. Of this there is no better proof than the practices of our legislatures and out courts. And yet, these practices are too often seen, even if advantageous, as setbacks to certainty and predictability. Missing is the realization that these standards, and these judicial practices, may be superior precisely because they enhance the certainty with which people can predict the consequences of their actions.

A final caveat: the extensive use of vague legal standards no doubt harbors dangers. Vague standards can easily mask arbitrariness, inconsistency, and injustice, and can also (of course) generate uncertainty. Their proper use requires good faith, professionalism, and intelligence, and therefore depends on a high caliber legal profession. But then again, it's hard to imagine a form of law (and of legal interpretation) that doesn't.

Freedom, Virtue and Practical Reason: the Present Relevance of the Differences between Ockham and St. Thomas

Diego Poole

I. Presentation

I intend to show to what extent, since the modern period, ethical reflection—including a great part of the Natural Law tradition—has been influenced by the thought of Ockham. I would like to focus attention on three fundamental concepts: freedom, virtue and practical reason; and to draw a comparison with Aristotilian-Thomistic thought.

In Ockham, we find the foundations of the modern notion of freedom as absence of determination. Ockham identifies freedom with will, and will with the pure capacity to choose between different options. Here, I shall attempt to highlight the contrast between this conception of freedom and that maintained by the Aristotilian—Thomistic school, according to which the foundation of freedom is a natural inclination towards ones own fullness.

With regard to virtue, Ockham loses sight of the idea that natural appetites are the subject matter of moral virtue. He reduces virtue to the habit of observing obligations or rules. Ockham transfers the moral centre of gravity, from the idea of integral human fulfilment, which is equivalent to happiness, to the idea of obligation. For Ockham, the natural bond between freedom and nature is broken, as much in God as in creatures.

Finally, Ockham conceives of practical reason as the activity of the intellect that brings the operation of moral norms into effect. I try to show the great difference between that idea and the notion of practical reason developed by Aristotle and St. Thomas.

In sum, I aim to emphasize the need to rehabilitate the study of Ockham, in order to understand to what extent certain fundamental ideas that have been ascribed to the Natural Law tradition are nothing more than adulterations made by Ockham, who projected them on the modern thought, as if they were the classical moral notions.

II. The Freedom (Liberty) of Indifference

For Ockham, will is not—as St. Thomas said—the passion for good or the rational appetite.

> I call freedom, says Ockham, the power that I have to produce indifferently and in a way contingent on different effects, that in such a way I could cause an effect or not cause it without producing any change outside of this power (Quodl. 1, q. 16).

In Ockham, the act of will, in order to be free, does not have to be provoked by anything, but only by one's own decision. In fewer words, unlike the Aristotilian—Thomistic tradition, Ockham does not conceive the act of will as a natural response to the "call of good".

Ockham loses sight of a fundamental theory of Thomas, namely, that the natural inclination of man to happiness is in the background of all decisions. For St. Thomas, if man didn't have a radical appetite for happiness, he would not elect absolutely anything: if we can elect something, it's because previously and naturally we desire happiness. For Aquinas, *the desire for happiness is not just an option among others: it is the foundation or the cause for whatever option.* Certainly, Ockham admits that in us exists the inclination towards happiness, but—according to him—we continue being completely free to want or not want happiness, the same with the ultimate end or the very existence: we are free to accept these inclinations or to refuse them.[1]

The difference is radical with respect to St. Thomas: for Aquinas, the inclination towards happiness, that is, towards personal fulfillment, is the same source of freedom and of moral life. For him, will was considered exactly as *the rational appetite for fulfillment*, appetite which is nourished by the impulse of the rest of the natural appetites (nutritious, sexual, etc.) in their path towards happiness (not in vain were they considered like *semina virtutum*, like the first sign of morality). For St. Thomas we are free, not in spite of these inclinations, but because of them.

Instead, for Ockham freedom comes before natural inclinations, to the point that man is freer as he becomes more impassible (the better with which he resists his natural inclinations). With that in mind, natural inclinations will not be the foundation of morals, but rather realities of material or biological order, that remain outside the reign of morality, and that are more of an impediment than an assistance in exercising free will. Will is considered, therefore, as a power that is completely independent of the body. Again body is seen in a platonic style: the body is seen as a jail for the soul. And soul, at the same time, is not conceived as *the form of an organic body* (as

---

[1] «..*voluntas pro statu isto* [*estado mortal*] *potest nolle ultimum finem sive ostendatur in generali sive in particulari. Quod probatur sic. Illud potest esse nolitum quod intellectus potest dictare esse nolendum. (Hoc paret de se). Sed intellectus potest credere nullum esse finem ultimum sive beatitudinem, et per consequens dictare finem ultimum sive beatitudinem esse nolendum. Secundo sic. Quicumque potest nolle antecedens potest nolle et consequens. Sed aliquis potest velle non esse. Igitur potest beatitudinem nolle quam credit consequi ad suum esse. Secundo dico quod intellectu iudicante hoc esse finem ultimum, potest voluntas illum finem nolle: quod probatur. Quia potentia libera est receptiva actuum contrariorum: qua ratione potest in unum et in reliquum. Sed voluntas tanquam potentia libera est receptiva nolle et velle respectu cuiuscumque objecti. Si igitur potest in velle respectu Dei: eadem ratione potest in nolle Dei....*» *IV Sent. q. XIV D.*

English: I'm saying that will in this state (mortal) can not want the ultimate end, whether it be presented in general or in particular. What I propose is this: it's possible to not want what intelligence can order no wanted. This is evident in itself. But intelligence can believe that there is not an ultimate end nor beatitudo and, in consequence, order that it wouldn't want the ultimate end or the beatitudo (Said). In other words: whoever that can no want the previous can not want the upcoming. But, whoever can not want to exist. He can, then, not want the beatitudo that believes consequently to his existence. I say, in second place, that (even) if intelligence judges that such a thing is the ultimate end, will can not want this end. I demonstrate this in this way: freedom is capable of contrary acts; for this reason it can establish itself in one sense and also in another. Now, will like free potential is capable of wanting or not wanting respect of whatever object. If will is, then, capable of wanting respect of God, for the same reason it cannot want the respect of God...

was seen by St. Thomas), but as a spiritual power *limited* by a body.

Morality, since Ockham, begins to be viewed as a limit to human freedom, imposed by the divine will. For Ockham, morality comes in order to limit a range of freedom which is originally undetermined, and that is only complete in God.

Morality receives from divine will its power to rule. Ockham introduces in the regime of morals the concept of obligation as the first principle of morality, an approach totally alien to Thomistic thinking.

Ⅲ. The Marginalization of Virtues

Once the moral category of natural inclination is suppressed, Ockham separates the free acts from the habits and, therefore, also from the virtues, understood as stable dispositions to act in a certain way. For Ockham, habits, in so far as they create certain dispositions to carry out certain acts, those habits diminish the power of selecting between opposing things, which is precisely, according to him, what defines freedom. An act realized under the impulse of habit seems less free than if it were realized through a purely voluntary decision. He who, for example, has the virtue of generosity and gives himself to others without effort, even joyfully, is seen as less virtuous than he who gives himself opposing his appetites. The difference is radical with respect to the thinking of Aristotle, for who the clearest indication that a virtue was deeply rooted in a person was the degree of joy with which he carried out the virtuous action. But, since Ockham, habits, and the virtues understood as habits, lose their own moral value and become simple customs, psychological mechanisms. All of that that limits our freedom (corporal regulations, inclinations of the senses, mental regulations) also limit the field of morality. The nominalist morality will not be, therefore, a moral of a subject that adapts himself each time better to the end (such was exactly the role of virtue in St. Thomas). For Ockham, morality will be evaluated only from each act independent of the other acts, comparing in each case the act with the will of God.

This does not mean that Ockham completely rejects the value of moral virtues. What happens is that, according to him, the only subject of virtue is will, not the appetites of the senses. Moral virtue is not—as in St. Thomas—a type of training of the appetites, but an exclusive quality of the will. "Solely the habit of will is 'properly' virtue". (III Sent. q. 10 D)

In Ockham *obligation is not derived from a natural inclination of man towards the fulfillment of his own form* (as St. Thomas would say) but has its origin in a command that, in a certain manner, is alien and independent from man. Obligation understood as such will be the constituent element and the same essence of morality. The moral life becomes *observance*, and the good man is defined as an *observant* man, and not as a fulfilled person. Doing good will be doing that which someone is obligated to do; and doing bad will be doing the opposite of what is obligated to do. « *Malum nihil aliud est quam facere aliquid ad cuius oppositum faciendum aliquis obligatur* ». (II Sent. q. 4 y 5 H)

Related, for Ockham charity isn't the virtue of the ultimate end, for that man loves passionately the union with God and with his fellow man, in which consists the blessed life. The love of God and love of the fellow man in God, does not have for Ockham the architectural and fundamental character of moral life, because such an attitude is only a response to a command of God, who moves man as though from a distance, through pushes. The communion that consists of the ultimate end is not seen by Ockham as something that naturally attracts man, like iron is attracted by a magnet.

Therefore it's clear that the center of morality, for Ockham, still isn't love, nor internal impulse, but an obligation, external impulse, surging from a purely divine will. For Ockham, man loves God in so that he observes obligation. In contrast, for St. Thomas love is that which moves you, and the obligation is not a load to bear, but *the effort of your own realization*. The same effort that any person puts forth to be attractive (with the goal of personal enjoyment and the enjoyment of others), is analogous to the moral effort needed to realize his or her own nature, by which man becomes good, enjoys and makes life pleasant for others. For St. Thomas, the first "moral obligation" is that of being happy, and becoming fulfilled. And this was not an egotistical vision, because St. Thomas conceived personal life as a part of a whole, that is the community of man; and the perfection of a part consists of being suitably disposed to the whole of which it is part.

Ⅳ. Natural Law and Practical Reason

Natural law is, for Ockham, a dictum of the reason that expresses divine will. Said as so wouldn't sound bad to scholastic thinking. But that dictum made by reason is not conceived as an intelligent response of man that selects the best ways for obtaining the ends that naturally already entice him. Reason only functions as "a conveyor belt" of the divine will, that is alien to the appetites of man. Ockham, completely confusing future generations, employs the expression "practical reason" for referring to the "application" that takes a man from the law to his actions. Aristotle practical reason—Aristotle is the man who invented this concept—was a completely distinct notion, because the major premise of practical syllogism was an attractive end; and his minor premise, the selection of the mean best suited to satisfy the enticing end. Aristotle practical reason doesn't consist of the application of the rule to the case, but in the selection of the most appropriate way to obtain an enticing end. Moreover, it was more appropriate to Aristotelic practical reason the creation of the law rather than its loyal observance.

For Ockham, it's not a work of practical reason the founding of moral laws in accordance with the end to which man naturally tends. "The function of practical reason (from Ockham)—says Pinkaers—consists essentially in the manifestation of the will of God, as it is expressed principally in Revelation, and in applying, after, those commands to a particular act through deductive reasoning and with the help of experience. This is principally the work of prudence".[2]

For Ockham, practical reason and prudence are, to say, purely intermediates between law and free will. Their function is to transmit rules, obligations. Such rules men know by the natural order of things « *stante ordinatione divina, quae nunc est* », that manifests the will of God, but is given that God can modify said order at any moment.

For Ockham an act is virtuous when will elects what reason interprets as divine will. For an act to be fully virtuous, it should be said by *recta ratio* and wanted solely because it is reasonable. « *Quia hoc est elicere conformiter rationi rectae: velle dic-*

---

[2] Pinkaers, Servais: *Las Fuentes de La Moral Cristiana*, Ed. Eunsa, Pamplona, 2007, p. 304.

tatum a ratione recta propter hoc quod est dictatum » (III Sent. q. 12 DDD).

All of this shows how *the "via moderna" has produced* a path that brings us to the theory of the Kant categorical imperative. The moralists who follow Ockham will use the term "conscience" to refer to prudence understood in this way: the conscience is conceived as that which, within the complex mind of man, is entrusted in transmitting to the case the orders and obligations born from the law.

Aristotle on Equity and Practical Wisdom: the Endless Task of Justice

Nuno M. M. S. Coelho

I. Introduction

In this article, we examine Aristotle's conception of equity (*epieikeia*) in its connection to the action and practical wisdom theory presented in *Nicomachean Ethics* (N. E.). Although Aristotle asserts equity is necessary just in some special situations (when the law is defective due to its generality), we try to demonstrate that equity cannot be understood as a virtue only eventually required, but every time the law must be used to solve a practical question. It is possible to affirm this from the Aristotelian reconstruction of the deliberation and decision process, and the strong relationship between justice and practical wisdom (*phronesis*) it suggests.

II. Equity as a Virtue and the Situation That Requires it

Some remarks are necessary before pleading our thesis. First of all, it is important to consider equity as a virtue.

The passages where Aristotle introduces the famous concept of equity deal with the problematic relations between justice and equity. The way his contemporaries use these words seems to keep some tension. Are justice and equity the same, or not? He starts from stating: "We have next to speak of equity and the equitable, and of their relation to justice and to what is just respectively", to finally conclude that "it is a special kind of justice, not a different quality altogether". He says (1137b...):

> It is now plain what the equitable is, and that it is just, and that it is superior to one sort of justice. And from this it is clear what the equitable man is: he is one who by choice and habit does what is equitable, and who does not stand on his rights unduly, but is content to receive a smaller share although he has the law on his side. And the disposition described is equity (...)[1]

Equity is not superior to justice at all, but to a certain sort of justice. Both equity and this other "sort of justice" belong to the same class. They are species of justice, and have the same nature: both are virtues. The species have the nature of the genus they fit in. In this sense, both are dispositions of a person used to acting in a certain way, who "acts by habit". A virtue is a good habit, a good custom, acquired through acting well in the past. At the same time, as a disposition, a virtue is a good habit that enables one to act well in the future.

A virtue can only be acquired through repetition. An ethical virtue is a good habit related to how a person desires. It will only be built throughout the experience of desiring. In the horizon of justice, one must deal with the desire of things useful for happiness. Being virtuous, here, is being in the habit of desiring neither too much nor too little of these goods, but just the ones that belong to us.

This is correct for any species of justice: for equity, and for legal justice—the other sort of justice to which equity is superior. They are both virtues, and, then, habits, dispositions acquired throughout the experience of situations where things useful for happiness (goods) are exchanged or distributed.

---

[1] Aristotle, *Nicomachean Ethics*, In Aristotle in 23 Volumes, Vol. 19, translated by H. Rackham. Cambridge, MA, Harvard University Press; London, William Heinemann Ltd. 1934.

Legal justice is the habit of taking, from the exchanged or distributed goods, the part that belongs to us, according to the law. The just man, considering justice as legal justice, is used to getting, for himself, the things the law indicates as belonging to him.

But the law may be wrong when it indicates what belongs to whom. In these cases, it is necessary to rectify the law, and then distributing or exchanging things must observe another criterion.

This is the kind of situation when/where equity must be exercised: the context of distributing or exchanging things necessary to success in life (*eudaimonia*), when a legal criterion does not seem to be correct. When the law does not fit the case, people involved in the case—or the judge—must find another answer to the question: which portion, from the distributed or exchanged things, belongs to each one involved? If the rule law were enough to establish that criterion, equity would not be necessary. But since the legal criterion is not correct, the equitable person must face the challenge to discover what belongs to whom.

One can build oneself as an equitable person (or not) in this sort of situation. It is not easy. Besides discovering that the law is not adequate to the case, he still must be successful in discovering the correct distributing or exchanging criterion by himself.

Some questions arise here, helping to think about the thesis we propose:

—How can one know that the law doesn't fit the case? It is the same as to ask: how can one be sure that the criterion established by law is not correct? How is it possible to recognize the cases where the law is defective?

—Once identified that the case requires "a special ordinance to fit the circumstances", which activity, power or capacity does make one able to find or to establish it by oneself?

—Doesn't that require discovering, in each and every situation, what is the right criterion (it means, the one which is adequate to the specific case), which must be contrasted to the legal criterion?

III. *Phronesis* and Aristotle's Intellectual Virtues Theory

These questions introduce a very important dimension of Aristotelian legal and moral theory, his theory of rational will, deliberation and practical decision. It is necessary to remember some topics in this field.

Different horizons to which human thinking can be directed establish particular tasks and patterns. Aristotle first distinguishes the thinking of things whose principles (*aitia*) are constant and eternal, from the thinking of things whose principles are contingent. The former is the horizon of *sophia* and *episteme*, while the latter is the horizon of *phronesis* and *thekne*.

Both *phronesis* and *thekne* are excellences in thinking of things whose principles are contingent. In this horizon, principles can vary exactly because they are placed by the person who thinks. Having *thekne* is being in the habit of thinking properly in the horizon of production. *Thekne* is the virtue which enables one to do good works, as a painter or an architect. The principle of producing lies on the human being (on the producer): the painting results from how the painter thought it. The goodness of the work is founded on the virtuosity of its author.

Phronesis relates to practical situations, where/when one must think about how to act (*praxis*). As a virtue, it enables one to deliberate correctly. Yet again the principle lies on the human being: the deliberation owes itself to the one who thinks it. The goodness of deliberation is founded on the virtuosity of the person who deliberates.

The practical situation offers two challenges to the person who must act. To be successful here, it is necessary to discover *what* to do, and *how* to do it. Being wise is not only discovering the right thing to do, but it is also finding the means to make it real.[2] This is true to *thekne* as well. A good artist is not only able to imagine the work, but to produce it as well.

How does one become *phronimos*? How does one become excellent in discovering what/how to do in practical situations? Being *phronesis* a virtue (an intellectual virtue) it is only possible to acquire it through the kind of situation where/when it can be exercised. Virtue only arises from exercising. *Phronesis* can only result from the experience of thinking the practical situations in which one has to deliberate and decide how to act. Deliberating well, one achieves the habit/disposition to deliberate well in future situations.

Aristotle emphasizes that each and any practical situation is marked by particular circumstances which make it singular. The right thing to do cannot be determined without a attentive awareness of the situation in its peculiarity. It can only be discovered in the concrete context of acting. That's why ethical theory (and the law, we can tentatively add) cannot offer more than general indications to the person who must act—as suggesting to research the mean (*mesotes*) in acting. But Aristotle, as an Ethics teacher, cannot indicate where the mean is in general, exactly because it can only be determined in the horizon of the case.

Being wise involves being capable of realizing and unifying certain facts the senses notice as a (practical) situation which requires acting. It always requires a special consciousness of its relevant and singular circumstances, as a condition to correctly establishing the measure of the desire. Acting well means desiring not too much nor too little, and this correct measure of desire is always related to the case.

The just man, in a general sense, desires the mean in the different horizons of life. This task also arises when we talk about justice in its particular sense, when the person must deal with his/her wish for external goods, and the exigency for taking for oneself not too much or too little from them arises.

---

[2] It clarifies how we understand the question of means and ends in the Aristotelian Ethics. Practical reason is always an effort to think ends and means of acting. The establishment of *eudaimonia* as the end of human life does not eliminate the question about the end of each and any action that projects the human being towards happiness. It is true that the end of each action (the answer to the question: what should I do now?) is a means related to *eudaimonia* as the final end (that is the same as to asking: what should I do now in order to get *eudaimonia*?). In this sense, the end to achieve in each situation is simultaneously a means to *eudaimonia*. It is an end-means, while *eudaimonia* is an end in itself. But being an end-means is still being an end.

Aristotle stresses it, indicating the various aspects of situation one must attend to in order to act justly.[3] It is still cleared by the connection between justice and voluntariness (1135 a):

> Such being an account of just and unjust actions, it is their voluntary performance that constitutes just and unjust conduct. If a man does them involuntarily, he cannot be said to act justly, or unjustly, except incidentally, in the sense that he does an act which happens to be just or unjust. [2] Whether therefore an action is or is not an act of injustice, or of justice, depends on its voluntary or involuntary character.
>
> (...) By a voluntary action, as has been said before, I mean any action within the agent's own control which he performs knowingly, that is, without being in ignorance of the person affected, the instrument employed, and the result (for example, he must know whom he strikes, and with what weapon, and the effect of the blow; (...) Or again, a man may strike his father without knowing that it is his father, though aware that he is striking some person, and perhaps that it is one or other of the persons present; and ignorance may be similarly defined with reference to the result, and to the circumstances of the action generally. An involuntary act is therefore an act done in ignorance (...).

As being virtuous (just in the general sense) and being just (in the particular sense) involve discovering the right mean which is always related to the case (the mean will vary according to the implicated persons, things, resources, time, place and other circumstances of the case), we should conclude that just obeying to the law can't be enough for acting well, because the rule of law never considerers the particular circumstances of the case, but can only mention a type of situation.[4] Law

---

[3] NE, 1131a: "Again, equality involves two terms at least. It accordingly follows not only (a) that the just is a mean and equal [and relative to something and just for certain persons], but also (b) that, as a mean, it implies certain extremes between which it lies, namely the more and the less; (c) that, as equal, it implies two shares that are equal; and (d) that, as just, it implies certain persons for whom it is just. 3. [5] It follows therefore that justice involves at least four terms, namely, two persons for whom it is just and two shares which are just. 3. [6] And there will be the same equality between the shares as between the persons, since the ratio between the shares will be equal to the ratio between the persons; for if the persons are not equal, they will not have equal shares; it is when equals possess or are allotted unequal shares, or persons not equal shares, that quarrels and complaints arise."

[4] 1135 a: "The several rules of justice and of law are related to the actions conforming with them as universals to particulars, for the actions done are many, while each rule or law is one, being universal."

may be eventually adequate to the case, but it may not to be. How can one conclude about this, without researching the mean by oneself?

It is not possible to be virtuous—just—without exercising equity. It is needed even to conclude that the rule of law, in that circumstances, really fits the case.

IV. *Phronesis* and Ethical Virtue as A Common and Endless Task

The specification of the type of situation where *phronesis* can be exercised shows the inner connection between this intellectual virtue and the ethical virtues. The situation where one must be wise (*phronimos*) is exactly the same where one has to deal with desiring and passion, and so must be just, courageous or generous. Having *phronesis* is being in the habit of thinking the situations where one faces the challenge to build oneself as character.[5]

It is not possible to be ethically virtuous without being wise, as the process that conduces to ethical virtue (acting well) requires the exercise of that intellectual virtue. This rises from the traits which distinguish the practical situation where acting is required, and the task to desire correctly comes up.

The difficulties involved in acting well arise from another order of consideration yet. Acting well requires not only *knowing* the right thing to do, but it especially depends on *desiring* it. Thinking and desiring (the rational and the appetitive dimensions of the soul) must be unisonant. Knowing the right thing to do is necessary to acting well, but is not sufficient. If desire doesn't embrace it, the person simply doesn't act like the reason suggests, as only desire (as something that happens in the irrational dimension of the soul) can move the animal the human being is.

If desire is not well habituated (it means, if the man has not a good character, in the moral sense), it will hardly attend to the counsel presented by the reason.

Linked to the task to build oneself as character (acquiring ethical virtues through desiring well), is the task to build oneself as a wise person. Besides the ethical virtues (dispositions/habits related to how one desires), the challenge of

---

[5] That's why it is impossible to understand *phronesis*, as described in Book VI, without connecting it to the description of ethical situations presented throughout the five previous Books of N. E.

eudaimonia depends on the construction of dianoethical virtues.

It requires finding the mean of desire in each and every situation, from the consideration of its particular circumstances. That is the job of *phronesis*, which must collaborate with desiring in the human developing into a happy person.

Being virtuous is not only being in the habit of acting in a predetermined way. The middle way can't be predetermined. The virtuous person does not simply act as she/he has acted, or as the law rules. As situations vary, the mean (the right thing to do) can vary, and one must be prepared both to finding it (being *phronimos*) and to desiring it (being virtuous in the ethical sense). The desiring dimension of the soul must be ready to embrace the middle way the rational dimension indicates. That means being equitable; as the middle way is not necessarily the mean assigned by law, the virtue of justice in its higher sense enables the person (the equitable person) to desiring the mean established by the practical reason, from the perception of the case in its particularity.

This leads to understand how being just (and virtuous in general) is an endless and difficult task. It always involves the work of finding and desiring, here and now, the adequate mean. Standing in justice requires a permanent effort to be equitable.

Balancing and Legitimacy: the Reflections on the Balancing the Legal Principles

Hannele Isola-Miettinen

I. Introduction

One could say that in the modern legal world the legal decision-making or "legal reasoning" in Courts and other authorities is more often the "balancing" than purely the simple "subsumption"—styled statute interpretation in its nature.[1] For example, in Finland or in Sweden[2] one important factor in this respect has been the development, due to the membership in the European Union. Namely, EU-law is more or less defined to be "legal principles". Along the legal theoretical literature the le-

---

[1] Aleksander Peczenick, *On Law and Reason*, Springer, 2009, p.14.

[2] For example, Jörgen Hettne in his study *Rättprinciper som styrmedel. Allmännä Rättprinciper in EU:s Domstol*, Norsteds Juridik, 2008, illuminates very well the effects the EU-law has had in legal system of Sweden.

gal principles are generally defined to be one important "source of law" in EU-law.[3] For example, Armin von Bogdany in the article "Doctrine of Principles" writes about the "doctrine of principles" and enshrines the function of the doctrine of principles.[4] Along Armin von Bogdany the doctrine of principles refers to "a systematic exposition of the most essential legal norms of the European legal order" in EU-law context. Along Armin von Bogdany the legal principles possible increase the rationality of the problem solving in the legal context, they create and secure the transparency and the coherence of the law. The legal principles are a kind of "framework of orientation" that is helpful in the Union's fragmented legal order. And importantly, Armin von Bogdany writes: "These principles can fulfil the function of 'gateways' through which the legal order is attached to the broader public discourse. A doctrine of principles has the task to prepare and accompany this process."[5]

II. Legal Principles?

This state of affairs obliges us to ask, how should we understand "the legal principles" in legal reasoning? Should we understand them to be an independent norm-type? Or should we think, that the legal principles are integrated into the system of law, so that legal principles are so called system principles? And, that legal principles are not the independent norms, like the rules are, but only the interpretation norms, in their nature. As we well know, that discussion on "rules and princi-

---

[3] Hettne Jörgen, *Rättprinciper som styrmedel. Allmännä Rättprinciper in EU:s Domstol*, pp. 41—43, pp. 45—46. Also, in Wennerström, "principles as substantive components in EU law", in Erik O. Wennenrström, *The Rule of Law and the European Union*, Uppsala, 2007, pp. 125—135. About legal principles, see Craig, Paul—de Búrca, Grainne, Craig, Paul—de Búrca, Grainne: *EC-law. Text, Cases & Materials*, Oxford, 2007, p. 73, p. 277 and p. 383, see p. 268, where "direct effet" is called doctrine. Also J. H. H. Weiler, *The Constitution of Europe. "Do the New Clothes Have an Emperor?" and Other Essays on European Integration*, Cambridge University Press, 2004, pp. 19—25, speaks about the doctrines. General principles are independent source of EU-law, see analysis in T. C. Hartley, *The Foundations of European Community Law, An Introduction to the Constitutional and Administrative Law of European Community* (sixth ed.), 2007, p. 131 and p. 221. Norbert Reich, *Understanding EU-law: Objectives, Principles and Methods of Community Law*, 2005, pp. 14—15.

[4] Armin von Bogdany, "Doctrine of Legal Principles Jean-Monnet" Working Paper 9/03, *Max Planck Institute for Comparative Public Law and International Law*, pp. 5—8.

[5] Ibid., pp. 5—8.

ples" by Ronald Dworkin has been inspirited European legal theorists since 1960's. That debate is unsettled and still disputable question in the legal theoretical literature. Instead of going more deeply to that discussion, one tries in this article to grasp the "the legal principles" in EU-law. One reflects first the legal principles in the case law of the European Court of Justice (ECJ). After that one focuses the legal principles on the theoretical level by reflecting 1) the balancing activity of "the legal principles" and 2) the legitimacy demand the balancing activity and legal principles in this respect cause.

Thus, the legal principles are several. For example, along Kaarlo Tuori there are found several typologies of the legal principles like: 1) the decision-making principles, 2) the interpretation principles, 3) the general principles, 4) the principles of sources of law, 5) the background principles of legislation or so called system principles. Tuori writes that the mentioned typologies are not independent, anyhow. In the legal practices the same principle (like fairness-principle) can be used sometimes as a decision-making principle, and sometimes as a interpretation principle.[6] The focus in this article is on some important EU-law "right" principles. In the EU-law it is used the term "rights" in very many and quite unclear meanings. For example, the so called "four Community freedom"—rights are very different kind of rights from the rights called "human dignity" or "privacy" rights, for example. There are several questions one has to reflect and refine theoretically in this theme: how to distinct those several rights as rights, how to define the content of rights, and how to balance those rights like the "four Community freedom" rights with the other rights? This article is not going to those questions, anyhow. One takes in this article such starting point that the rights or even some of them, are supposed to be merely legal principles than rules, in their nature.

III. Balancing—What the Balancing Means?

What do we do mean with the term "balancing"? What are we "doing" in our minds when we are balancing? What kind of mental activity "the balancing" presupposes? First, let's see what the balancing means in the general language? The "bal-

---

[6] Kaarlo Tuori, *Oikeuden ratio ja voluntas*, Vantaa, 2007, pp. 150—151.

ance" in general language refers, among others, "to apparatus for measuring weight, scales, counterpoise, weight balancing another, equilibrium, equipoise either physical or mental, harmony between parts of a whole, proportion, weigh in the mind, one possibility against another, equal in weight". One could say, on the ground of this kind of the definition that the balance is merely the result that we are trying to achieve by the balancing activity. The balancing takes place in our minds. In the legal context and in the legal reasoning there is not available any "apparatus" for measuring the weight or value of different aspects, of course. The balancing is just trying to achieve "equilibrium" or "harmony between parts of whole", in its nature.

1. Expanded set of premises?

In legal literature the term balancing is not the new concept. In legal theoretical literature the "balancing" (or the "balancing and weighing"[7]) is well known term in the discussion concerning legal interpretation. In the introduction we stated that balancing is legal reasoning in its nature, but not the legal reasoning in its traditional narrow meaning. Usually we discuss on legal reasoning that refers to the legal interpretation in so called "hard cases" in the context of the statute interpretation. In the "hard case" the decision does not follow from a legal rule and a description of facts but from several expanded set of premises.[8] So, the problem in hard cases is "expanded set of premises".

Anyhow, should we define the balancing to be one form of "legal reasoning" where the problem is on the "expanded set of premises"? The legal reasoning refers to the "arguments" we have to give for our decisions. The arguments consist of "reasons" for decisions. And, we think that those reasons are the "justifications" for the decisions we make. Arguments, reasons and justification are needed in the legal reasoning that takes place 1) inside of the frames of statutes or 2) in the situation we balance the "expanded set of premises". It is possible to think, that the legal principles are "expanded set of premises" in frames of statute law or should we think and accept that the legal principles are one "independent group of norms", like the "rules" are.

---

[7] For convenience, instead of the term "weighing and balancing" it is used in this article the term balancing describing that activity that the "weighing and balancing" term refers.

[8] Peczenick, *On Law and Reason*, p. 15.

2. Pluralism law?

The fact is that "legal pluralism" has got more room in the European legal systems. It has caused the effect, that it is not more possible to pack all the several values of the pluralistic society into the legislation beforehand, in the legislative processes. The European Union is one very interesting example in this respect of the pluralism. Namely, in the preamble of the Charter of Fundamental Rights of European Union the aim of Union is "to share a peaceful future based on common values". And, in the same preamble it is articulated, that "The Union contributes to the preservation and to the development of these common values while respecting the diversity of the cultures and traditions of the peoples of Europe as well as the national identities of the Member States" and their organisations on all levels. As we can see, the European Union really manifests at the same time "common values" and "respecting cultural pluralism and pluralism of traditions". For example, Weiler writes that "The potential conflict of values emerges, classically, in response to the question: which standard of protection should the European Court adopt?"[9]

In this article it is argued that legal pluralism is one important reason why the premises outside the frames of statutes are more and more important "source" in the legal interpretation. The balancing activity necessarily takes more room in the legal reasoning. As we have already mentioned, one such more important source of the law is the rights: basic rights or human rights or the Community freedoms rights. The positions taken in legal theory to the "rights" varies. For example, Aulis Aarnio sees that "basic rights" should be seen in legal interpretation primarily as a question "inside of statute law" and the rights should be seen as a question of "all things considered"—discretion.[10] Aarnio in his legal theory rejects the idea of the principles as the independent norm type. Along Aulis Aarnio the difference between the rules and principles is more gradual than qualitative.[11] Anyhow, is possible to argue that those "extended premises", that are also found "outside the frames of the statute

---

[9] Weiler, *The Constitution of Europe. "Do the New Clothes Have an Emperor?" and Other Essays on European Integration*, p. 109.

[10] Aulis Aarnio, *Tulkinnan taito. Ajatuksia oikeudesta, oikeustieteestä ja yhteiskunnasta*, Vantaa, 2006, pp. 316—317.

[11] Ibid., pp. 304—305.

law" allow more discretion to judges and other authorities.

In this discussion we come to the problem of the legitimacy of the balancing activity: how we legitimate those "extended premises" that are necessarily needed in the discretion of the judges and other authorities? There is no simple solution. But it is important even to try to find the understanding of that difficulty. Namely, the strictly positivistic worldview does not help us to see the problems of the modern law, like the challenge of the legal principles and the balancing. As Mark Van Hoecke interestingly writes the legal thinking is the need of the legal theory and an external point of view that is necessary in the interdisciplinary research. The internal point of view is narrow and the legal education very rarely offers some methodology for carrying out the comparative in interdisciplinary research.[12]

Ⅳ. The Object of the Balancing?

In European Union the European Court of Justice (ECJ) in its case-law is balancing the different kind of "rights" against each others. As we know, the basic rights and human rights are sometimes count to be moral rights, in their nature. In this respect and on the theoretical point of view, it is difficult to define the status of so called "Community for freedom" rights in relation to those basic rights or to the human rights. We leave unsettled question if the so called "Community for freedom" rights merely belong into concept of the policy goals, than into the morally coloured categories of basic rights or human rights? As told before, this article is not furthering that epistemological discussion on various rights in the discipline of moral philosophy.[13] Sieckmann's definition in this question of the rights is very satisfactory. Sieckmann in his writings calls "basic rights" as *a priori* rights, because their existence is possible to establish independently and before the legislation procedure.[14]

---

[12]　Mark Van Hoecke, *Law as Communication*, Oxford, Hart Publishing, 2002, p. 81.

[13]　The very interesting discussion in this respect is gone in the discipline of moral philosophy in the study, *Principled Ethics: Generalism as Regulative Ideal*, Sean D. McKeever and Michael R. Ridge ed., Oxford University Press, 2006.

[14]　Jan-Reinard Sieckmann, "Basic Rights in Model of Principles", 30—36, Rights, Proceedings of the 17th World Congress of the International Association for Philosophy of Law and Social Philosophy (IVR) Bologna, June 16—21, 1995, Vol 1, ed. Rex Martin & Gerhard Sprenger, ARSP—Beiheft Stuttgart, 1997.

1. Omega case: community freedoms v. human dignity

In the preliminary ruling case *Omega* the company (named *Omega*) asked if the prohibition order, that the Bonn police authority was issued against it, was compatible with the Community law. The lower German courts had already dismissed *Omega*'s appeal in that case, where the police authority had forbidden *Omega* "playing at killing people", among others. Lastly, the Federal Administrative Court in Germany (Bundesverwaltungsgericht) took the view" that, under the national law, *Omega*'s appeal must be dismissed. However, in this case the Federal Administrative Court saw it uncertain whether that result is compatible with the Community law and Treaty articles on the freedom to provide services and the free movement of goods. The Federal Administrative Court said that lower instances were right saying that *Omega*'s killing game constituted an affront to human dignity, a concept established in the German Basic Law. The Federal Administrative Court saw that this kind "fictious acts of violence for the purposes of the game" are infringing "human dignity" that is constitutional principle.[15]

2. Restrictions in earlier case-law

The main principle in European Union law is, that the "rights based on Common market freedoms" must not be hindered. The national Court in this case referred to the earlier ECJ—case law, where ECJ has been elaborated the acceptable criteria for restrictions for the one of the Community freedoms, for freedom to provide services:

—measures are justified by overriding reasons relating to public interests,

—they are such as to guarantee the achievement of the intended aim,

—they do not go beyond what is necessary in order to achieve it.[16]

The Federal Administrative Court said that it has received the impression from earlier case law that ECJ no longer adheres strictly to the need for that common conception to restrict the freedom to provide services.[17] One reason to that impression

---

[15] C-36/02 Omega Spielhallen—und Automatenaufstellungs-GmbH v Oberbürgermeisterin der Bundesstadt Bonn, [2004] ECR I-9609, paras 5,10,11,12.

[16] C-36/02 Omega (n 15), para 14 and para 36.

[17] C-36/02 Omega (n 15) paras 14,15.

was due to the discussion gone on over the status of the national basic rights and the human rights in EU-law (like in the *Scmidberger* case).

Advocate General Stix-Hackl in the case *Omega* payed attention to the increasing need to settle the relation between so called fundamental rights and the Community freedom rights. Advocate General Stix-Hackl referred to the importance of the fundamental and human rights saying that they have "legitimating" effect in the modern world law. Advocate Stix-Hackl saw, that those principles should be taken into the account when the EU—legislation in interpreted. But, Stix-Hackl stresses that the fundamental rights are not only interpretation principles but "more" than just interpretation principles.[18] Interestingly, Advocate Stix-Hackl tries to found the solution through reconciling. With referring to the formula adopted in the earlier Schmidberger judgement, Stix-Hackl proposes: ... "how the requirements of the protection of fundamental rights in the Community can be reconciled with those arising from a fundamental freedom enshrined in the Treaty." This reconciling is taken by Stix-Hackl after the careful conceptual analysis.[19]

3. Reason: activity in this case is affront to the human dignity

Anyhow, in this case *Omega* ECJ took such a position, that the Community law does not preclude an economic activity consisting of the commercial exploitation of the games simulating acts of the homicide from being made subject to a national prohibition measure adopted on grounds of protecting the "public policy" by the "reason" of the fact that that the "activity is an affront to human dignity".[20]

4. Protection of fundamental rights justifies the restriction of Community freedom right

The ECJ structures its statement in *Omega* case to the earlier settled case law. Along the Court fundamental rights form an integral part of the general principles of law the observance of which the Court ensures. For that purposes the Court draws inspiration from the constitutional traditions common to the Member States and from the

---

[18] Advocate General Stix-Hackl C-36/02 Omega Spielhallen—und Automatenaufstellungs-GmbH v Oberbürgermeisterin der Bundesstadt Bonn [2004] ECR I-9609, passim.
[19] Advocate General Stix-Hackl (n 18), para 72.
[20] C-36/02 Omega (n 15), paras 34—35,39—41.

guidelines supplied by international treaties for the protection of human rights on which the Member States have collaborated or to which they are signatories. ECJ says that the European Convention on Human Rights and Fundamental Freedoms has special significance in that respect.[21] Court says that since both the Community and its Member States are required to respect fundamental rights, the protection of those rights is legitimate interest which, in principle, justifies the restriction of the obligations imposed by Community law, even under a fundamental freedom guaranteed by the Treaty.[22]

5. There is no general common restriction criteria shared by all Member States

As already mentioned, in this case it was referred to the earlier established ECJ case-law that allows Member State to restrict its interests on the basis of the different kind of provisions. ECJ stresses now in this *Omega* case that it has not established any general criteria in order to define the restrictions for exercise of the economic activity.[23] With this general criterion ECJ wants to say that, it has not developed any general criteria on "a conception shared by all Member States" concerning the restrictive measures:

> It is not indispensable in that respect for the restrictive measure issued by the authorities of a Member State to correspond to a conception shared by all Member States as regards the precise way in which the fundamental right or legitimate interest in question is to be protected....[24]

ECJ stresses that although it has in the earlier case law mentioned such reasons like moral, religious or cultural considerations which allow all Member States to make some restrictions, ECJ says that it was not its intention, "by mentioning that common conception, to formulate a general criterion for assessing the proportionality of any national measure which restricts the exercise of an economic activity".[25]

---

[21] C-36/02 Omega (n 15) para 14 and para 33.
[22] C-36/02 Omega (n 15) para 14 and para 35.
[23] C-36/02 Omega (15) para 38.
[24] C-36/02 Omega (n 15) para 37.
[25] C-36/02 Omega (n 15) para 37.

6. European Court of Justice in Omega—case gave more value to human dignity than Community freedom right

In this case *Omega* the ECJ saw that the proportionality principle has taken into account and it accepted that "human dignity" is more important value than "common market freedom". In *Omega* case the special feature is that the "human dignity", which was restricting the freedom to provide services, did not correspond to the conception shared by all Member States. The system of the protection that is different from that adopted by another Member State, is not excluded. The ECJ states that the protection in this *Omega* case is not against the "proportionality" principle and it is not unjustified restriction on the freedom to provide services.[26] Important aspect in this case was that "human dignity" is guaranteed also in EU-law system as a general principle of law. The ECJ said that the protecting human dignity is with no doubt compatible with EU-law. Moreover to that, ECJ refers to that, the principle of respect for human dignity has a particular status as an independent fundamental right.[27]

In this preliminary case *Omega* ECJ balanced two kinds of rights: 1) the "Community freedom to provide services", based on the EU-law and, 2) the "human dignity". In fact, in the preliminary ruling case *Omega* the ECJ balanced the common values of the EU-law.

As Advocate General Stix-Hackl says, the concept of the human dignity is difficult: it is impossible to equate the substance of the guarantee of human dignity under the German Basic Law with that guarantee of the human dignity, as recognised in the Community law. That is why Advocate General Stix-Hackl proposes, that the circumstances of the "public policy" invoked by the Member State, is to be analysed and to be justified from point of view of the importance and scope of the human dignity in the Community legal order. Namely, the "public policy" discretion departs from the EU-law and in that discretion the EU-law sets to the Member States strict limits. But lastly, Advocate General sees the human dignity as one important common "value"

---

[26] C-36/02 Omega (n 15) paras 36—38.
[27] C-36/02 Omega (n 15) para 34.

between the Member State and EU-law.[28] Very great importance in the ECJ courts discretion must give to investigations of the Advocate General Stix-Hackl, who analysed carefully the concept of "human dignity" in German Basic law and in the Community law. In the balancing activity of the ECJ the important aspect anyhow was that it accepted the restriction of Community freedom rights on the basis of the Community law, not because of the provisions of German Basic Law. The important aspect is that the ECJ clearly included in this case *Omega* the "human dignity" into the Community legislation and into the fundamental rights which the ECJ protects.

As Morijn analyses, in this case *Omega* ECJ developed a Union law approach to deal with Member State's invocation of fundamental rights as laid down in national constitutions for the purpose of derogating from the common market freedoms of European Community. Along Morijn the methodology by which fundamental rights and common market rights are "balanced" in European Union law goes to the core of how the fundamental rights are valued within the field of application of European Union law.[29] Weiler shows that that ECJ is tending to adopt so called "maximalist" approach as a standard of human right protection instead of the "minimalist" one because of the high level of protection.[30] As Hettne writes, ECJ has developed general principles by efforting to find support in Pan-European principles and legal traditions. It seeks guidance in international treaties on fundamental rights to which Member States have subscribed, like European Convention of Human Rights. If the Member States have acceded to such treaties the ECJ can assume that their content is in accordance with the Member States' legal systems and can allow the relevant provisions in the treaties serve as guidance for the development of EC—law. Hettne writes that the reference to the European Convention and other international treaties that are binding on Member States provides legitimate support for this legal development.[31] Where there is no guidance to be obtained from treaty text or from international treaties the ECJ resorts the comparative method. With that methods it aims to ascertain

---

[28] Advocate General Stix-Hackl (n 18) paras 92—93 and 98.

[29] John Morijn, "Balancing Fundamental Rights and Common Market Freedoms in Union Law: Schmidberger and Omega in the Light of the European Constitution", (2006) 1 *ELJ*, p. 15, p. 40, pp. 15—17.

[30] Weiler, *The Constitution of Europe. "Do the New Clothes Have an Emperor?" and Other Essays on European Integration*, p. 109.

[31] Hettne, *Rättprinciper som styrmedel. Allmännä Rättprinciper in EU:s Domstol*, p. 320.

what principles can be regarded as recognised by at least the great majority of Member States. The basis idea is that the principles derived in this way must correspond with the common constitutional traditions, and of course legal values, of the Member States.[32]

V. Who/Which Organ is Balancing Values?

As we can see in that *Omega* case, the "values" play a heavy weight in the balancing activity of ECJ. There is a good reason to pose the question, who/what organ in the society has the ultimate power to balance those values and to define which values are the common values in the society. In the *Omega* case, for example, along Morijn the ECJ defines the acceptability of the Community restriction in concern, but the substantial aspect of the reasoning was left to the Member State. The ECJ does not itself embark upon substantial verification on the basis on national law or on basis of law of the European Convention of Human Rights law. That is the methodology by which the Court of Justice now protects uncommon constitutional traditions of fundamental rights protection in European Union law.[33] Along the EU-law preliminary ruling system it is the national Court of Member State, and not the European Court of Justice, that always gives the final judgement in the single case. It seems that the substantial "balancing" of the legal principles takes place in the Courts of the Member States, not on the EU—court level. On the other hand, it is the ECJ that has developed and defined the most important principles of the EU-law, like the principles of the primacy and the supremacy[34] or defined the status of the "four Community freedom rights" in relation to the national legislations and the constitutions.

In the EU-law system usually the highest national Court is allowed to make the preliminary references to ECJ. In the so called "Grand Chambre" judgement *Tietosuojavaltuutettu v Satakunnan Markkinapörssi and Satamedia* reference for a prelimi-

---

[32] Ibid.

[33] Morijn, "Balancing Fundamental Rights and Common Market Freedoms in Union Law: Schmidberger and Omega in the Light of the European Constitution", pp. 34—35.

[34] Weiler, *The Constitution of Europe. "Do the New Clothes Have an Emperor?" and Other Essays on European Integration*, pp. 19—22.

nary ruling was made by Supreme Administrative Court in Finland. In that case the ECJ stated that the directives (directive on protection of individuals in processing personal data[35]) object to reconcile fundamental rights, and in this case the protection of privacy and freedom of expression, belongs primarily to Member State. "The obligation to do so lies on the Member States".[36] There are some cases where ECJ has expressly challenged the Member State to balance the legal principles. In this development it has been clearly empowered the status of the national courts of Member States, in relation to the national parliaments? The balanced legal principles in this mentioned *Tietosuojavaltuutettu v Satakunnan Markkinapörssi and Satamedia* case were:

—the "free flow of personal data"
—the "right to privacy"
—the "right to freedom of expression"

The implementation of the EU-law directives usually belongs to the national parliaments. In this case, and because of the reference for the preliminary ruling taken in the *Tietosuojavaltuutettu v Satakunnan Markkinapörssi and Satamedia*, the balancing task was practically directed to the Finnish national parliament which is obliged to "balance" in its legislative process certain of those fundamental rights in question: the protection of privacy and the freedom of expression. The ECJ states that the objective of the directive in the question is to permit the free flow of the personal data. In addition to that, the objective of the directive is to protect the fundamental rights and the freedoms of natural persons and in particular their right to privacy with respect to the processing of the personal data. The ECJ states that the objective cannot be pursued without having regard to the fact that those fundamental rights must in some degree be reconciled with the fundamental right to the freedom of expression. The article nine of the directive expressly refers to such a reconciliation. It is written into the preamble of the directive that the objective is to reconcile two fundamental rights, the protection of the privacy and the freedom of expression. The ECJ states

---

[35] European Parliament and Council Directive (EC) 95/46 on the protection of individuals with regard to the processing of personal data and on the free movement of such data.

[36] C-73/07 Tietosuojavaltuutettu v Satakunnan Markkinapörssi and Satamedia [2008], ECR, 16. december 2008, para 54.

that the obligation to do so lies on the Member States.[37] In Finland it is the parliament which implements the EU—directives. That is why the balancing activity to which ECJ refers, is thus supposed to take place in the legislative organ, in the national parliament. The activity of the national parliament is based on the system of the representative democracy. Because of that, the assumption in this case is, that national parliament in its legislative process is legitimating the balance of those fundamental rights. The assumption is based on the idea that the national parliament will in its rational discussion process balance those fundamental rights. In the Finnish legal system we still assume that it is "the legislation" given by national parliament, which legitimates the law in the society.

Some European legal orders have established the Constitutional Courts. In Finland it has not been established such a constitutional Court. The Finnish speciality is the Constitutional Committee which is functioning inside the parliament organisation. In Finland the constitutional problems, like balancing the basic rights, are usually solved "*a priori*" and "*in abstracto*" in Constitutional Committee. So, as a matter of fact, in this case *Tietosuojavaltuutettu v Satakunnan Markkinapörssi and Satamedia* the ECJ is, de facto, directing the instructions concerning the balancing activity to that Constitutional Committee of national parliament.

Along those instructions the ECJ says that the Member States for the purposes of that directive in question are required to provide for a number of the limitations in relation to the fundamental right to privacy (= protection of the data). The ECJ says in this case that those derogations must be made solely for journalistic purposes or the purpose of artistic or literary expression, which fall within the scope of the fundamental right to freedom of expression, in so far as it is apparent that they are necessary in order to reconcile the right to privacy with the rules governing freedom of expression.[38] Moreover, the ECJ articulates about "the importance of the right to the freedom of expression in every democratic society. Along the ECJ it is necessary to interpret notions relation to that freedom, such as journalism, broadly. Secondly, and in order to achieve a balance between the two fundamental rights, the protection of fun-

---

[37] C-73/07 Tietosuojavaltuutettu v Satakunnan Markkinapörssi and Satamedia (n 36) paras 52,53 and 54.

[38] C-73/07 Tietosuojavaltuutettu v Satakunnan Markkinapörssi and Satamedia (n 36), para 55.

damental right to privacy requires that the derogations and limitations in relation to the protection of data provided... must apply only in so far as is strictly necessary".[39] Anyhow, the problem is that the Constitutional Committee in Finland do not have any obligation or even the power to settle the concrete and individual cases. Those concrete individual cases are finally settled case by case in national Courts, of course. In its case law the ECJ leaves in the individual cases the discretion power to the national Courts. Also, in this case *Tietosuojavaltuutettu v Satakunnan Markkinapörssi and Satamedia* the national Court is the very instance which finally determines by its interpretation, what was the purpose of the activity in this case, if it was the disclosure of information to the public, opinions, ideas or not.[40]

Ⅵ. Theoretical Reflections on the Balancing the Legal Principles

Many theoretical problems have their inspirational origin in practical problems. So is the case in issue concerning the balancing of some EU—rights or right principles, too. There is the theoretical need to widen the approach to the law and to the legal problems from that purely internal point of view more towards the external approach and towards to the so called extended set of premises. Traditionally, for example the legal reasoning in Finland, has been mostly the legal statute interpretation, in its nature. And the statute interpretation has been occurred in the conceptual frames of those written statutes that are given by national parliaments in the legislative procedure. In addition to that, the legislation given by the national parliaments in the legislative procedure, has been the most important source of law in Nordic countries. One could argue that the legislative procedure has legitimated that legislation. The legitimation of law is based on the idea that the national parliament as a representative organ articulates "values" of the society and citizen into the legislation and the judges and other authorities have to follow those provisions and values in their legal reasoning.

Van Hoecke writes that the human right principles have been culminated in Hu-

---

[39] Ibid., para 56.
[40] Ibid., para 62.

man Right Declarations at the end of eighteenth century as a result of the rationalist natural law approach of modern times. After written into the constitutions and into the international treaties, the human rights have become the part of the positive law on a worldwide scale.[41] The challenge to "cultural" change in question of legal sources has been vast since 1990's. In many European countries, like in Finland, for example, the "legal culture" has been, and is still, undergoing deep changes. There is no doubt, that one great reason for this kind of challenge towards cultural change is the membership of the European Union and the EU-law. There may be several other reasons for this kind of change, of course. In this article the purpose has been to stimulate the discussion that concerns the "balancing" activity.

For example, in Finland one important departing point in legal decision-making is the avoidance of arbitrariness, in other words, "the judicial decision must be predictable". Aarnio, in his introduction to Aleksander Peczenick's study, "On Law and Reason" (2009) sees that "... predictability is one of the fundamental conditions of human activity".[42] In addition to that, general assumption is that the "judge must make his decision in accordance with law in force and, at the same time, take into the consideration the values that are generally accepted in society". This concept of legal certainty, along Aarnio, involves two central elements, "law and values or, in order to use everyday language, law and morality." Aarnio writes that to Peczenick the connection between the legal and the moral is the central problem. Aarnio is his introduction writes:

> The concept of legal certainty ties this connection with certain elementary and fundamental phenomena in society. The "alliance" between law and morality thus has deep roots in legal culture. For this reason, analysis of the background of legal interpretation is always, in a way, a culture analysis.[43]

As we well know the model for judicial interpretation is disputed. Some authors see that such a model cannot be proven, at all. It can only be more or less adequate. It is also important that theoretical constructs does not violate common usage

---

[41] Hoecke, *Law as Communication*, pp. 121—122.
[42] Peczenick, *On Law and Reason*, pp. 3—4.
[43] Ibid., p. 4.

of language, framework of behaviour or implicit expectations. Otherwise, as Aarnio writes, the construct cannot work in our culture.[44] For example, in Peczenicks model it can be distinguished two different types of justification 1) contextually sufficient justification and 2) deep justification, that in other words means the justification of the justification.[45] Peczenick is coping in his writings "a moral reason". Anyhow, it has been critically presented by some authors that Peczenick, for example in his doctrine of transformation, is mixing the law and morality together, which results ambiguity of the concept of law. Anyhow, this kind of approach typical to Nordic tradition sees the morality as an integral part of law.[46] In his thinking Aleksander Peczenick is value relativist, he sees that legal norm can be interpreted in more than one way. Opposite to Peczenick's approach, for example, Ronald Dworkin thinks that there is always one right solution. Dworkins problem is that the one right solution is not always found.[47] The legal principles are not the new invention in the legal theory. Ronald Dworkin probably is the most commonly cited author in the legal studies concerning the discussion on the theoretical difference between the "rules" and the "legal principles". The well known definition is that "Principles have a dimension that rules do not—the dimension of weight or importance". [48]

We know that vague words in law (in statutes) are "value-open" and that is why we have to precise the interpretation of those vague expressions. In this process, the answering to that the question in the concrete case, presupposes and depends on act of weighing and balancing.[49] One interesting question is the object of the balancing. Namely, in the balancing operation we are moving, one could say, outside the frames of the statute law and the rules. In balancing operations "the rights" and "the principles" seem to receive more importance? One question is: are "the principles" independent norm type or are they integrated into the legislation legislator have given? The problem of rights and the rights's relation to so called "model of princi-

---

[44] Ibid., p.5.
[45] Ibid., p.5.
[46] Ibid., p.8.
[47] Ibid., pp.8—9.
[48] Ronald Dworkin, *Taking Rights Seriously*, Harward University Press, Eighteenth printing, 2001, pp.26—27.
[49] Peczenick, *On Law and Reason*, pp.16—17.

ples" has been reflected among others by Jan-Reinard Siekmann in the article "Basic Rights in the Model of Principles" (1997). Sieckmann calls the basic rights as *a priori* rights because their existence is possible to establish independently and before the legislation procedure. Along Sieckmann the recognition of these kind of rights is not simple. Because rights are not necessarily established in legislation procedure, there must be some means how to recognize them to be valid law. Namely, such recognition is necessarily needed; it is the condition of the validity of legal norms. The normative sense of validity of law means that law is binding its addressees. Basic rights are presuppositions of the bindingness of the legal norms. One has to ask what is justifying the bindingness of the norms.[50] Interestingly, Siekmann sees that the model of principles is the model where the "definitive norms" are established as the result of the weighting and balancing principles. And, this correct result of the weighing and balancing procedure is not completely determined by the cognitive intersubjectively valid criteria. Sieckmann talks in this context and because of the legitimacy demand, about special autonomy rights: rights to moral autonomy, right to personal autonomy and about the right to participation in a practical discourse.[51] Sieckmann has elaborated "the model of principles" in his study "Regelmodelle und Prinzipienmodelle des Rechtssystems (1990). There is no agreement in legal theory that legal norms are divided into legal rules and legal principles. Sieckmann in his study "Regelmodelle und Princiepenmodelle des Rechtsystems" (1990) makes a division:

—The strong thesis of the division (Trennungsthese), that means the logical difference between rules and principles so, that the difference between them is not gradual,

—The weak thesis of the division, that means the gradual logical division between the rules and principles and,

—The thesis of the agreement that there is no logical difference between rules and principles but both groups of norms have similar features.[52]

The criterias of this logical division concern the use (Anwendung) of these two groups of norms or the situation of the norm collision. The logical division concerns

---

[50] Sieckmann, "Basic Rights in Model of Principles", pp. 30—36.
[51] Ibid., pp. 30—36.
[52] Ibid., p. 53, refers to Alexy and to references concerning the Dworkin/H. L. A. dispute.

the structure and form (geltungsoperators) of those group of norms.[53]

One problematic area is "legal principles" and merely "unwritten legal principles". It is nor very rare to find the legal principles in the judgements given by the European Court of Justice, for example. As told earlier, one interesting group of legal principles are the fundamental rights and the Community market freedoms in European Union context. That was state of affairs in *Omega* case. The legal base of community market principles is in the Treaty provisions and in the case law elaborated by ECJ.

VII. System Principles or Independent Legal Principles?

In the European legal system legal principles are not usually seen as independent category of norms. Anyhow, the European legal system is the system of the legal principles, that is one independent source of law. One could ask, is it possible to claim the rights on the basis of the legal principle? One possible way to divide legal principles is to distinguish 1) structural principles and 2) ideological principles.[54]

1. Ideological Principles

Ideological principles are mostly used, *contra legem*. That means that the ideological principles are used as the correcting principles.[55] Purely ideological legal principles do not have institutional support. They are the application of non-legal values or norms by the courts.[56] Along Mark Van Hoecke ideological principles are generally applied only to restrict the application of some legal rules. They correct the applications of rules, which in some specific circumstances are considered to be

—clearly unfair,
—unreasonable,
—unacceptable,

When compared with some commonly accepted ideological point of view. Just only when it is clearly seen the conflict with some commonly accepted moral or politi-

---

[53] Ibid., p. 53.
[54] Hoecke, *Law as Communication*, pp. 170—171.
[55] Ibid.
[56] Ibid., p. 164.

cal principle, will the legal rule be disregarded and the non-legal principle be applied in the form of a, newly formulated, general legal principle. Mark Van Hoecke stresses heavily that ideological principle always functions as the correcting principles.[57]

2. Structural Principles

Structural principles are derived from legal system itself. Thus they have fairly strong institutional support. Along Van Hoecke structural principles are mostly used *praetor legem*. Structural principles are mostly guiding principles, with broad scope.[58] In comparison to the ideological principles, the structural principles have often broader scope and this makes the structural principles function as guiding principles.[59] Structural legal principles are the hidden axioms of the logical structure of the legal system or some branch of it. Their acceptance is necessary or at least desirable for the optimum coherence of this legal system. Structural principles are implicitly present in the legal system. They are present at the system, even if the legislator may never have been clearly aware of them. For example,

—the binding force of international treaties can be deduced from the nature of these agreements, in international law the principle *pacta sunt servanda* can be considered to be logically necessary *a priori* which is inherent in the concept of treaty, in a sense it is the Grundnorm of international law,

—the prohibition of economic discrimination and the principle of economic liberty follow from the foundations of the EU legal order.

Ⅷ. Legitimacy Aspects of Balancing Legal Principles

As Mark Van Hoecke writes is his book "Law as Communication" the traditional representative democracy idea legitimising the law is obsolete. Mark Van Hoecke departs from the argument that law creation can not be seen any more as a one-way process: " citizens-elections-parliamentary legislation-judicial application ". The

---

[57] Ibid., pp. 164—165.
[58] Ibid., pp. 170—171.
[59] Ibid., pp. 164—165.

complexity of law and the society has made such a theme obsolete. Van Hoecke writes that the strengthened role of judges and the establishment of supranational courts have weakened the role of parliaments to the advantage of the governments and the administrations. Van Hoecke proposes to develop new theories, both descriptive and normative theories on the law and the democracy. [60]

The most interesting point has been to reflect is it really the national parliaments which do have the autonomy and the decision making power over basic rights of its citizens. Or it is really regional/international organisations and their Courts which define the ultimate "values" used in the human rights balancing. How do the citizens of the European Union legitimate these kinds of human rights and the restrictions on them written into the international conventions/treaties? As seen in the case *Omega* or in *Tietosuojavaltuutettu v Satakunnan Markkinapörssi and Satamedia* which has been studied earlier in this paper, it is the national court of Member State, that finally gives the decision in the individual case. This not the whole truth—the ECJ has defined, among others, the doctrine of supremacy over national legislations and constitutions. There is no doubt that the role of the courts and judges in modern legal world has in some extent weakened the position of the national parliaments. But as we have seen in the case *Tietosuojavaltuutettu v Satakunnan Markkinapörssi and Satamedia*, in the national parliament whose obligation it is to legislate and balance on basis of the relevant EU—directive about the human rights that the directive protects.

When reflecting the balancing the human rights originated from the treaty/convention sources one has to keep in mind what Dahl in his book "On Political Equality" (2006) says: 1) international systems make decisions that bear important consequences for, among others, citizens in democratic countries, 2) many of the decisions resulting from international systems lead to highly desirable results, 3) yet the decisions of the international systems are not and probably cannot be made democratically. For example, the European Union is not the worst case in this respect of democracy aspect in the world. Anyhow the democratic deficit is unsolved problem in European Union, anyhow. For example, it has been proposed to establish the right-

---

[60] Ibid., p. 10.

based democratic model to legitimate the European Union law[61]. Should the European Union Charter of Fundamental Rights serve the better and more acceptable basis for that law legitimation and legitimacy issue? In the article "Still in Deficit: Rights, Regulation, and Democracy in the EU" written by Richard Bellamy, it is focused the important tension concerning so called democracy deficit in European Union. Along theorists there are seen two lines in democracy question: 1) a right-based view of democracy and 2) public-interest view of delegated democracy. Along the conclusions of Richard Bellamy there are problems in both alternative tensions, the standard versions of the democratic deficit in European Union retain their force. Bellamy sees that at the moment the lack of common "demos" is obvious and this means the weak possibilities to develop the majoritarian decision-making democracy in European Union. One question is, would it be the better possible solution, instead of the European Union majoritarian democracy, be the enhancing the democratic accountability within the established democracies of the Member States?[62] Namely Robert Dahl sees very serious problem in the majoritarian democracy itself. There is the gap between the ideal and actual. Dahl is counting the ideals that belong to the democracy: effective participation, equality in voting, gaining enlightened understanding, the final control of the agenda, inclusion and fundamental rights.[63] The fundamental rights along Dahl means that each of the necessary feature of an ideal democracy prescribes a right that is itself a necessary part of an ideal democratic order: a right to participate, a right to have one's vote counted equally with the votes of others, a right to search for the knowledge necessary in order to understand the issue on the agenda, and a right to participate on a equal footing with one's fellow citizens in exercising final control over the agenda. Democracy consists, the Dahl says, "not only political processes. It is also necessarily a system of fundamental rights".[64].

Now Dahl comes to the interesting question; if we assume that membership in the demos and necessary political institutions have been satisfactorily established, what limits may properly be placed on the authority of the demos to enact laws, and

---

[61] Bellamy, "Still in Deficit: Rights, Regulation, and Democracy in the EU", (2006) 6 *ELJ*, pp. 725—742.
[62] Bellamy, "Still in Deficit: Rights, Regulation, and Democracy in the EU", pp. 726—728, p. 742.
[63] Robert A. Dahl, *On Political Equality*, Yale University Press, 2006, pp. 9—10.
[64] Ibid., p. 10.

more concretely, on the authority of the majority of the members of the demos?[65] Dahl answers that the fundamental rights necessary to democracy itself cannot legitimately be infringed by majorities whose actions are justified only by the principle of equality. Dahl writes that it would be inconsistent with democratic beliefs then to impose limits on the authority of a majority to undertake actions that would destroy an institution like freedom of speech that is necessary if a democratic system is to exist.[66] There are many aspects in this problem of course. It is not the irrelevant question who or which organs legislate, decide or balance the substantial content or limits of the "rights" on "rights principles" in the society.

Ⅸ. Conclusions

The balancing as a human mental process is the giving "weight and values" to several legal competing legal principles. The balancing activity is usually taking place outside the frames of the statute law. The balancing the legal principles are not the measuring, anyhow.

In the legal theory there is a unsettled dispute, if there are found the independent legal principles or not. The solution is difficult. Sieckmann has developed principled model for the balancing idea. The legal principles have in legal theory divided, for example, into structural legal principles and ideological principles. The function of the ideological principles is to correct law. Structural principles are merely integrated into the system of law as guiding principles.

New legitimating models are needed in legal theory because of the increased legal pluralism. Mark Van Hoecke neglects the connection of the modern law to the state. Van Hoecke sees that the model of the traditional representative democracy as a theoretical starting point is obsolete because the weakened position of national parliaments. Mark Van Hoecke proposes to invent new descriptive and normative theories in the area of law and democracy.

Balancing has strengthened the status of the judges and the courts. One problem is who/which organs legitimate "balanced" law in the modern legal world. The ECJ

---

[65] Ibid., p. 15.
[66] Ibid., p. 17.

is both indirectly or directly balancing the law applied in the EU Member States. In the European Union context we can find the difficult and still unsolved, so called, democratic deficit problem. For example, Dahl sees that the decisions of international systems are not and probably cannot be made democratically. The discussion about the majoritarian democracy idea is not simple, anyhow. We should count fundamental rights into the democracy idea, too. The balancing the legal principles seem to be one invention in this problem.

The Principle of Proportionality

Marijan Pavčnik[*] Friedrich Lachmayer[**]

No argument is independent in the sense that it would by itself substantiate a legal decision. Each argument has to be applied within a context and with regard to other arguments by which we define our attitude to particular elements of legal decision-making and to the relations between these elements. If any argument is considered to be particularly lacking in independence, it is certainly the principle of proportionality. In the literature the standpoint has been formed that the principle of proportionality "neither embodies nor protects independent values; it is a measure to protect recognized rights or interests, or a measure for a necessary coordination of such interests or rights in situations when they cannot be realized simultaneously and completely, and therefore they all have to be limited to a certain extent".[1]

If it were concluded there from that the argument of proportionality is just an "instrumental principle", the range of this principle would be misconstrued at the

---

[*] Author of the text.
[**] Author of the visualisation.
[1] Dobrinka Taskovska, *Proportionality as a General Principle of Law (Its Articulation in Legal Theory and Comparative Public Law)*, Dissertation: Ljubljana, 2000, p. 295.

very beginning. The principle of proportionality interpreted as a relation (pp) is based on the *right balance* between too much and too little, therefore it *a priori* dissociates itself from a teleological relation (te) with an end (value, criterion) that is self-sufficient and from a measure that is blind and obedient.

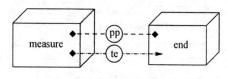

Figure 1

Of main importance is the question of how to reach the right balance between conflicting rights and legal duties, goods and burdens, an end and the measures needed to achieve this end.

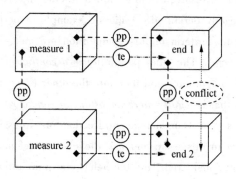

Figure 2

The principle of proportionality must take into consideration that all rights and legal duties are correlative. Correlation always *also* means that the subject of a right must not go beyond its limits (i. e. the limits of legal entitlement), whereas the subject of a duty is always entitled to require of others that they not hinder him in his behaviour.[2] This aspect of correlation has often been disregarded or at least not sufficiently considered, even though it is the one aspect that requires that our behaviour be legally harmonized with the behaviour of others in a suitable manner.

---

[2] Marijan Pavčnik, *Teorija prava (Theory of Law)*, 3rd edition, Ljubljana, 2007, p. 206.

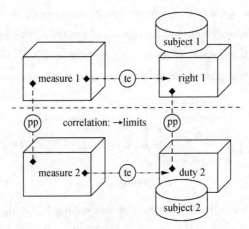

Figure 3

The first issue to be resolved is to establish whether the conflict of two or more legal behaviours is legally permitted. A classic example of permitted competition is *loyal competition*; if the criteria of this competition are met, the behaviour of the competing parties is *legal*. The other possibility is *a conflict of two rights*, of which one is stronger (more important) and therefore the other (less important) one has to give way to the right that is *legally more important in concreto* (e.g. in a case when the protection of privacy is stronger than the freedom of expression). Further in this article we shall return to this issue and ask the question of how to solve a conflict when a basic (constitutional) right and the behaviour of an authority (the state) collide.

The third possibility is the conflict of two rights that have to coexist and live together. With rights of this kind, nobody can refer to the principle that he who exercises a legal right harms no one (*Qui suo iure utitur, neminem laedit*). Whoever acts in such a manner does not base his behaviour on the right; his behaviour is just a "seeming exercise of a right" (Art. 7/3 of the Slovenian Code of Obligations[3]) and is completely forbidden (a pure legal violation).

A general legal principle is that the rights of legal subjects are limited by the equal rights of others (see Art. 7/1 of the Slovenian Code of Obligations; see also

---

[3] Art. 7/3: "It is a seeming exercise of a right if its subject acts with the exclusive or evident intention to harm someone."

Art. 14/2[4] and Art. 15/3[5] of the Constitution of the Republic of Slovenia). If individual subjects exercise their rights in such a way that they partly or completely intrude upon the rights of others, the intruding right has to be limited with regard to its content and the previous state has to be re-established if this is possible in view of the nature of the intrusion. It is of key importance for the issue in question to find the appropriate criterion for defining the contents of the conflicting rights, to limit them and thereby delimit them from each other. In principle, it can be said that the right of a subject may not go beyond the limit enabling the other subject to activate and exercise his right *within the scope of equal quality*. If a subject goes beyond this limit, this is already an *abuse* and no longer the exercise of a right.[6]

The criterion of a *scope of equal quality* is a rather loose one and has to be operationalized in view of the natures of both rights and of the concrete circumstances. The Code of Obligations requires that rights have to be exercised in accordance with the basic principles of the Code (e. f. with the principle of loyalty and good faith) and with their intention (see Art. 7/1). Court practice has already established criteria such as the intention (i. e. the end) of the right, acting with loyalty and good faith [e. g. *Venire contra factum proprium (nemini licet)*], justified interest, the non-existence of a benefit (i. e. a legally protected benefit), the nature of the matter, an appropriate measure (the least burdening measure that still completely puts a legally protected interest into effect), the "equal weapons" of the parties (to a procedure), groundless protraction of the procedure (an abuse of procedural rights!), etc. Of *special consequence* among these criteria are the legally protected interest or the legally protected benefit (as the intention of the right), the principle of the least burdening behaviour and the proportional consideration of the other person with respect to his right. If two persons that have a right to water are in conflict and one of them is a farmer and the second one is the owner of a holiday home, they are both

---

[4] Art. 14/2: "All are equal before the law."

[5] Art. 15/3: "Human rights and fundamental freedoms shall be limited only by the rights of others and in such cases as are provided by this Constitution."

[6] I deal with the abuse of a right in the article "Abuse of a Right" [in: *Archiv für Rechts- und Sozialphilosophie—Beiheft* 67 (1997), pp. 64—71] and in the article "Missbrauch des subjektiven Rechts. Beitrag zum Verständnis des subjektiven Rechts und dessen Natur" (in: *Verbot des Rechtsmissbrauchs. VI. Rechtstage von Luby*. Bratislava, 2001, pp. 69—143).

entitled to water, yet to a *different quantity* of it, because the farmer's right is of a different *quality* than the right of the owner of the holiday home.

In all these cases one is on very sensitive ground because one cannot avoid valuing and nuancing the matter in view of the concrete circumstances. The task of court practice is to standardize these cases and to add to the already formed types of behaviour new ones or at least subclasses of typical constituent elements. This entails a standardization that should express the right balance between the conflicting rights: the balance is right if it is possible to find a quantitative proportion enabling the co-existence of both rights with regard to their quality.

This is also true, *mutatis mutandis*, of the basic (constitutional) rights which the state power may intrude upon or limit, and of legislative (law-giving) regulation in general, which may not groundlessly restrain rights and increase legal duties. In foreign theory (e. g. in Germany[7]) and in foreign court practice (e. g. before the Court of Justice of the European Communities[8] and before the European Court of Human Rights[9]), the principle of proportionality[10] has been established, which has also been adopted by the Slovenian Constitutional Court.[11] The *principle of proportionality* has *two stages*. In the *first stage* it has to be established whether the end (i. e. the intention) of the legal act (e. g. a statutory provision) and the measure that is to bring the end into effect are legal (especially whether they are in accordance with the constitution and statute). This is the so-called "legitimacy test", which should examine whether "the end pursued by the state is legitimate i. e. factually justified" and "whether the measures applied by the state are as such legally permissible".[12] Then follows the *second stage*; its task is to examine the quality of

---

[7] See e. g. Karl Larenz, *Methodenlehre der Rechtswissenschaft*, 5th edition, Berlin (etc.), 1983, p. 392; Horst Dreier, in Horst Dreier (editor), *Grundgesetz. Kommentar I*, 2nd edition, Tübingen, 2004, p. 128; and Bodo Pieroth, Bernhard Schlink, *Grundrechte. Staatsrecht II*, 18th edition, Heidelberg, 2002, p. 65.

[8] See e. g. Paul Craig, Gráinne de Búrca, *EU Law*, 3rd edition, Oxford, New York, 2003, p. 371.

[9] See e. g. P. van Dijk, G. J. H. van Hoof (editors), *Theory and Practice of the European Convention on Human Rights*, 3rd edition, The Hague, 1998.

[10] See e. g. Nicholas Emiliou, *The Principle of Proportionality in European Law. A Comparative Study*, London (etc.), 1996.

[11] See e. g. *OdlUS* (*Decisions of the Constitutional Court of the Republic of Slovenia*) III, 62; IV/2, 67 and 131; VI/1, 69; IX/1, 21; X/2, 192; XI/1, 49 and XII/1, 7.

[12] Lovro Šturm, in: Lovro Šturm (editor), *Komentar Ustave Republike Slovenije* (*Commentary of the Constitution of the Republic of Slovenia*), Ljubljana, 2002, p. 55.

the measures and to establish whether a suitable (legally correct) proportion exists between the end and the measure (the so-called principle of proportionality in the strict sense of the word). The *quality of the measures* is examined by the criteria of the suitability (Germ. *Geeignetheit*) and necessity (Germ. *Erforderlichkeit*) of the measure. A measure is *suitable* if it is at all likely to achieve the end (since otherwise it is a false measure). And a measure is *necessary* if it is the minimum intervention necessary to reach the end (the principle of the mildest or the least burdening measure [13]). The essence of the second stage is the *proportionality in the strict sense of the word*, which is centred on the proportion between the end and the measure; the end that is pursued should not require disproportionate (excessive) burdens in comparison with the benefit gained. A classic example is a dangerous brain test for establishing insanity; in the concrete case of a petty criminal offence, such a test was rejected as being *disproportionate* to the end because ten per cent of such tests result in physical disorders (in some cases even serious health problems). [14]

The principle of proportionality is of a *gradual nature* and plays an important role in legal practice. In Slovenia, it is the Constitutional Court that applies it rather intensively and has already adopted several precedent decisions in this regard. [15] The fundamental reservation is contained in the so-called *legitimacy test*, which can be misleading. The misunderstanding could be in that the Constitutional Court adopts the role of the legislature and judges whether the legislature's end is legitimate. The Constitutional Court does not have this competence; it is "only" within its power to establish whether the legislature's (the law-maker's) end is constitutional (also legal if an executive regulation is in question). *Hassemer* would probably say that it has to

---

[13] Ibidem, p. 56.

[14] *BVerfGE* 16, p. 194.

[15] See the examples cited by Šturm (fn. 12), p. 62. See and cf. also Dragica Wedam Luki?, "The Principle of Proportionality in the Case Law of the Constitutional Court of the Republic of Slovenia", in: *Human Rights, Democracy and the Rule of Law. Liber amicorum Luzius Wildhaber*, Edited by Stephan Breitenmoser, Bernhard Ehrenzeller, Marco Sassòli, Walter Stoffel, Beatrice Wagner Pfeifer, Dike, Nomos: Baden-Baden, 2007, pp. 1599—1617.

be an end within the limits of constitutional democracy.[16]

The Slovenian Constitutional Court has expressed its standpoints about all the elements of proportionality. The first one is the contentious expression "legitimate ends of the legislature".[17] The expressions *legitimate end* (*aim*) and *legitimate interest* have to be understood as a *legal* (*constitutional*) *end* (*interest*). It means that the legitimate (substantiated with regard to its content) end is achieved in a legal (constitutional) way. In another decision (that has already been cited), the Constitutional Court was more definite and explicitly stated that it must be a "constitutionally permissible end".[18] A further element refers to the constitutionality (legality) of the measure that should realize the constitutional (legal) end. A classic example would be violating the torture ban (*an unconstitutional measure*) in order to achieve a constitutionally permissible end.[19] Furthermore: a measure is unsuitable (*suitability of the measure*) if, for example, "the limitation of the choice of the location of an attorney's office" is determined as "a measure to safeguard the impartial deciding of judges and state prosecutors".[20] Furthermore: a measure is not *necessary* if the statute, "for safeguarding people's security, only foresees detention and does not alternatively define any less strong preventive measures that would still safeguard people's security".[21] And furthermore: the criterion of the right balance requires that the end and the measure are *balanced*; the balance is upset when "the height of the rent for reserved parking lots (...) is evidently disproportionate to the value of this exclusive use of a public good".[22]

---

[16] See Winfried Hassemer, "Ustavna demokracija (Constitutional Democracy)", in: *Pravnik*, 58 (2003), pp. 4—5, pp. 207—226. See also *OdlUS* IV/2, p. 131, p. 487: "The application of the principle of proportionality means that before ordering the intervention in a constitutional right it must be assessed: firstly, whether the intervention is at all suitable for achieving the desired, *constitutionally permissible end* [this standard first step in assessing the permissibility of an intervention may be omitted when the court imposes detention because the assessment was already performed by the legislature; italics added by M. P.]; secondly, whether the intervention is really necessary ('unavoidable') such that the desired end cannot be achieved in any other manner...".

[17] Cf. *OdlUS* IV/2, p. 67, p. 121.
[18] *OdlUS* IV/2, p. 131, p. 487.
[19] See Boštjan M. Zupančič, in: *Commentary* (fn. 12), p. 209.
[20] *OdlUS* V/1, p. 27.
[21] Ibid., p. 40.
[22] *OdlUS* VI/1, p. 21. See also *OdlUS* X/2, p. 193.

The balance between the end and the measures brings us back to the core of the problem—to the correlation of legal relationships, which is a central feature of law.

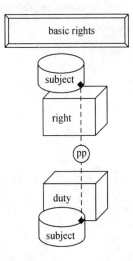

Figure 4

One can speak of correlation in connection with a *mutual interdependence of behaviour* of two or more legal subjects. Correlation also exists between subjects of rights and subjects of rights whose content is of a dutiful nature (e. g. relationships between parents and children) as well as subjects of legal duties that are connected to each other with regard to their content. The correlation of duties especially pervades administrative law and public law in general. In public legal relationships, citizens are often subjects of legal obligations (e. g. tax obligations) that are in keeping with the "entitlements" of state authorities to provide that the citizens fulfil their obligations. The "entitlements" of state authorities are, by their content, legal duties that state authorities cannot relinquish without being affected by sanctions.[23]

The correlation of legally possible actions (the correlation of rights, the correla-

---

[23] In Anglo-Saxon legal theory the correlation and opposition of "rights" and "legal duties" were perspicaciously discussed by the U. S. legal theoretician Wesley Newcomb Hohfeld (1879—1918). Hohfeld's monograph is very important, yet it has to be considered that it is written in a language that differs from that of European continental theory of law. See Wesley Newcomb Hohfeld, *Fundamental Legal Conceptions*, New Haven—London, 1964, p. 35, p. 65.

tion of rights and duties, the correlation of duties) cannot avoid this relation to the other. The quality of law always depends on how these relationships are established *de iure* and *de facto*.[24] On a suitable occasion also this side of law will have to be uncovered and appropriately analyzed.

---

[24] The value background of such correlation in law is discussed by Louis E. Wolcher, *Law's Task: The Tragic Circle of Law, Justice and Human Suffering*, Aldershot, Burlington, 2008.

Towards a Hermeneutical Approach to Legal Metaphor*

Alberto Vespaziani

This paper examines the importance of metaphor in legal discourse. It discusses the reasons for the lack of specific studies of the relevance and structure of metaphors in the law in general, and in Italian constitutional law in particular. Three claims are put forward: 1) legal discourse is constituted by a mobile army of metaphors; 2) there is no such a thing as a non-metaphorical legal language; and 3) strong ideological prejudices work against a recognition of the basically metaphorical nature of legal concepts. The paper examines the rhetorical conception of metaphor and then summarizes the three dominant theories of metaphor: semantic, structuralist and hermeneutic, and argues that only a hermeneutical approach can grasp and fuse the cultural horizons of inherited, metaphorical, interpretive traditions. It concludes that comparative law, with its work of translation, is an excellent standpoint for examining the values underlying legal metaphors.

---

* The Italian version of this paper was written for inclusion in the volume *Scritti in onore di A. A. Cervati*.

Ⅰ. Law and Metaphor

"Normative language is metaphorical"[1]. With these words, Italian scholar Alessandro Giuliani called upon legal scholars to venture into the field of metaphor studies, in order to deepen their awareness of legal terms and doctrines. Legal practitioners and scholars work with words to resolve disputes and pursue justice, but also to obscure, mislead and promote unspoken interests. The inevitable, sometimes insidious use of metaphor reflects the ambiguous nature of law and of language; metaphors can be used to further communication and clarification, but also to produce disinformation and confusion:

> The entire history of legal thought could be studied from the standpoint of language as a sequence of metaphors: it would be enough to examine any ordinary controversy in legal scholarship to see that the different arguments are conditioned upon the accepted metaphors, analogies and the use of examples. We can see the demonstration of Blumenberg's theory of the existence of key terms as *absolute metaphors*, which cannot be further broken down into logical terms: the impossibility of agreeing on the meaning of the term "law" is an example of this fact. The task of legal analysis is the correction of metaphors and the clarification of language.[2]

Giuliani thus suggests that legal experts ought to study rhetoric. The purpose of this is not to sharpen our oratorical skills or our ability to employ seductive metaphors; the purpose in studying rhetoric derives from the fact that legal language is intrinsically metaphorical, for better or for worse. The ethical task of legal thought thus consists in uncovering the ideological projects hiding behind—or even within—legal metaphors.

The classic objection to the discussion of metaphors, raised by the traditional, professional, legal academic is that they are the concern of literature, maybe even

---

[1] A. Giuliani, *La « nuova retorica » e la logica del linguaggio normativo*, RIFD, 1970, p.379. See also *Logica* (*teoria dell'argomentazione*), Enc. Dir.

[2] A. Giuliani, *La « nuova retorica » e la logica del linguaggio normativo*, RIFD, 1970, p.379.

philosophy, but have nothing to do with the life and practice of the law.[3] Underlying this belief is the assumption that legal language may be cleansed of the sentimental imperfections of poetry and literature, of the base materialism of economics and of the senseless mental gymnastics of theory and philosophy. But this assumption is not only epistemologically naïve; it also serves ideologically to justify the legal profession's project of manipulating the sentiments and interests of others for economic gain, political power and social privilege.

The legal thinker that instead accepts Giuliani's suggestion to travel down the uneven path of clarifying, reframing and correcting legal metaphors will have to critically examine the values underlying legal terms and expressions, as well as the power relationships implicit in legal doctrines' choices of words. For example, if we ask "why do we say 'sources of law'? Why do we use this hydraulic metaphor?", we will begin to analyze the presumed nature of the "product" of a legal norm: the norm originates somewhere underground, and then gushes out of a kind of mountain spring (a pristine place presumably, this site of political power condensation), ready to be bottled and delivered to judges, government lawyers and other faithful servants passively carrying out orders received from on high, without asking too many questions about their content or value. Notice how the hydraulic metaphor of the source gives rise to the imperative and anthropomorphic metaphor of the "law-maker", which leads to the bureaucratic and military metaphor of the civil servant. Similar considerations follow when expressions like "head" of state, constitutional "organ", electoral "body" (to mention a few of the most obvious organic metaphors in constitutional law) are viewed through the lens of metaphor studies.

Another classic objection against the study of metaphors appeals to the correctness of the literal meaning as opposed to the vague arbitrariness of metaphor. A precise, professional judge might argue that when it comes to interpreting the meaning of

---

[3] The provocative aspect of metaphor studies has been well-described by Severo Sarduy, "Metafora al quadrato su Góngora", in G. Conte (ed.), *Metafora*, Milan, 1981, p. 187: "Metaphor is the point at which language's plot thickens, the point at which it takes on such importance as to render the rest of the sentence flat and innocent. Like a yeast bubbling at language's continuous surface, metaphor confers a certain degree of denotative purity on all that comes near it. Purity. Let us underscore the moral implications of this word: metaphor as extraneous to the "nature" of language, like an illness; it impugns every rhetorical figure, dragging it into the forbidden zone, so much that Saint Thomas boasted of having no use for metaphors at all".

a legal provision, we must focus on the original meaning of the text as intended by the legislator. This anti-hermeneutical presumption, which denies the relevance of interpretation in service to an idea of objective meaning and thus denies the interpreter's own subjectivity, can be found in every legal culture, in every area of the law, at every level of legal sophistication and at every ideological extreme.

The myth or prejudice of literal interpretation is perhaps one of the most ideologically resistant of metaphors: its simple suggestion of an uncontaminated source of meaning in a distant act carried out by someone else, and its call to neutralize the subjectivity of decision-making, serve every jurist's latent desire to escape from freedom. Now, from the hermeneutic perspective, it is clear that there is literally no such thing as a literal interpretation. The sequence of l-e-t-t-e-r-s does not produce nor does it evoke meaning. Literal interpretation suggests that normative language is like a mosaic, while a hermeneutical approach sees it more like an organism. To willfully not see the forest for the trees, as the literal approach does, means to effectively deny that a qualitative, ideological or strategic choice is being made. As anyone who has crossed the shadowy valley of translation knows, translating a phrase from one language to another is nothing like taking apart a mosaic and putting the pieces back together somewhere else; translating a legal concept from one cultural context to another is more like transplanting a whole tree in a different soil. Still, the belief persists that behind words there are things, that behind logic there is being, that behind abstract norms there are concrete interests, that behind appearance there is substance, that behind form there is content and that behind the metaphor there is the concept. These beliefs are so archetypal, and thus so deeply-rooted (and as such, they are advantageous, reassuring and forgiving) as to force a hermeneutical approach to justify itself again and again, to set forth its particular assumptions and announce its particular critical project: normative language is metaphorical language; metaphorical language is ordinary language; and metaphor is not just a rhetorical form but the very structure of language. Moreover: the supposed opposition between a literal interpretation and a metaphorical one is itself a metaphor, the metaphor of language as a series of letters.

While metaphor studies have flourished in semiotics, semantics, comparative literature, rhetoric and political theory [4], Italian legal scholarship has not developed a specific interest in this subject. Beyond the comments of Giuliani, there have not been searching examinations of the use of metaphor in Italian constitutional discourse. The reasons for this prolonged silence can be located in: 1) the prevalence of positivism, which conceives of legal language as normative and imperative; 2) the prevalence of formalism, which seeks to purify forms of their content; and 3) the decline of rhetoric as an allied field of legal education. According to Giuliani:

> The devaluation of metaphorical and figurative language has become a tacitly accepted dogma in modern legal thought; and it is the intersection of profoundly contrasting positions, which depart from realistic or nominalistic assumptions. This devaluation is connected to the corruption of the authentic dialectical tradition. At its root is a nervous suspicion of opinion and of any analysis that is not based on compelling, demonstrative evidence. This has produced the reduction of prescriptive language to imperatives, because only these forms of prescription seem to belong to the domain of the rational. The other forms remain irremediably consigned to the domain of persuasion, rhetoric and the irrational.[5]

According to Giuliani, the decline of metaphorical language in the law is the consequence of our expulsion from the dialectical paradise of antiquity. Apart from his dubious conceptualization of an "authentic" dialectical tradition (a curiously undialectical image of dialectic, so insulated from discussion, purified of contamination and restored to its ancient and original splendor), one can ask whether Giuliani's Aristotelian conception of metaphor is satisfying, or whether instead the reduction of metaphor to a mere trope is not partially responsible for its consequent marginalization.

From the perspective of Italian constitutional scholarship, the first instinct of one who sets out to discuss metaphors and law is to put forward the canonical (as well as metaphorical) *excusatio propter infirmitatem*: the field is too vast to try to cover it in the scope of this examination, a complete study of the role of metaphors in law has yet to be written, the literature is endless. Richards, after having evoked the intuitions of Shelley and Bentham, and having "glanced for a moment at these deep

---

[4] V. F. Rigotti, *Metafore della politica*, Bologna, 1989 and *Il potere e le sue metafore*, Milan, 1992.
[5] A. Giuliani, La « nuova retorica » e la logica del linguaggio normativo, RIFD, 1970, p. 382.

waters into which a serious study of metaphor may plunge us", located in the "fear of them [...] one cause why the study has so often not been enterprising and why Rhetoric traditionally has limited its inquiry to relatively superficial problems". [6] Moreover:

> The neglect of the study of the modes of metaphor in the later 19th Century was due, I think, to a general feeling that those methods of inquiry were unprofitable, and the time was not ripe for a new attack. I am not sure that it is yet ripe in spite of all that Coleridge and Bentham did towards ripening it. Very likely a new attempt must again lead into artificialities and arbitrarinesses. If so, their detection may again be a step on the road. In this subject it is better to make a mistake that can be exposed than to do nothing, better to have any account of how metaphor works (or thought goes on) than to have none.[7]

I would like to put forward a few considerations in favor of a hermeneutical conception of metaphor in legal discourse. The assumptions from which I proceed are that: law is language, legal language is metaphorical, metaphorical language is ordinary language, legal language is as specialized as it is common, the meaning of legal discourse can be grasped only through a process of interpretation, metaphors work by essentially transacting between contexts, and comparative law—whose basic and difficult task is translation—is in a privileged position to study their function. Metaphor studies and translation studies intersect in the zone of critical hermeneutics: in contrast to the other approaches to metaphor, only hermeneutics is concerned with the historical embodiment of the subject which is interpreting a text. It takes two ideas to make a metaphor, and so there are no metaphors in the dictionary, but only in discourse. The function of a critical study of metaphor is to suggest a technique for liberating ourselves from the defects of the interpretative traditions that we have received but not interrogated.

This paper will proceed in several steps: first, I will summarize the origins of the reduction of metaphor to a rhetorical trope, then I will discuss three main currents in modern metaphor studies: the semantic paradigm, the structuralist paradigm

---

[6] I. A. Richards, *The Philosophy of Rhetoric*, Oxford, 1936, p.91.
[7] Ibid., p.115.

and the hermeneutical paradigm.[8]

I intend to argue that (1) language in general, and thus legal language in particular, is constituted by a mobile army of metaphors, by metaphors that point to other metaphors; (2) a non-metaphorical language does not exist; and (3) there are a series of prejudices, laden with ideology and false conscience, that resist this hermeneutical vision, such as the illusions: of an objective substance underlying subjective appearances, of an ontological reality underpinning linguistic formulations, of an economic structure giving rise to a legal superstructure and of a scientific rigor that is superior to a poetic indeterminacy.

II. The Origins of a Rhetorical Conception of Metaphor

"Men in fact are affected in the same way by style as by foreigners and compatriots. So the discourse must be made to sound exotic; for men are admirers of what is distant, and what is admired is pleasant".[9] In his work on rhetoric Aristotle casts an image of distance as a vehicle of eloquence. Of all the brilliant figures that can be expressed in speech, metaphor stands out for its iconic ability to "make visible". Aristotle believes that metaphor translates speech into images, making it more beautiful and thus more persuasive. This is the basis of an ornamental conception of metaphor: metaphors can bring inanimate things to life. Finding beautiful metaphors means knowing how to see and how to grasp the similarity between different things. Metaphors have a manipulative character, which leads Aristotle to advise drawing them "from related but not obvious things... Most witticisms are also produced through metaphor and an additional illusion; for what the hearer hears becomes clearer to him through its being the opposite to what he thought, and the mind seems to say, 'How true, and I was wrong'"[10]. Metaphor's persuasive effect comes from manipulation, and Aristotle sets forth a taxonomy to organize this: "metaphor is the

---

[8] Like all classifications, this one is ultimately arbitrary and subject to criticism. As Barthes reminds us, "The passion for classifying always seems Byzantine to one who does not share it [...] and yet it is usually normal. The taxonomic option implies an ideological one: there is always a *placed* in the place of things: *tell me how you classify and I will tell you who you are*", R. Barthes, *La retorica antica*, Milan, 2006, p. 53.

[9] Aristotle, *The Art of Rhetoric*, H. C. Lawson-Tancred (tr.), London, 1991, Chapter 3.2, 1404b.

[10] Ibid., 1412a.

imposition of a name on another thing: either the name of the genus applied to the species, or the name of the species applied to the genus, or the name of one species applied to another, or an analogy"[11].

Metaphor emerges from this analytical reduction as a figure of speech, supported by a prejudice in favor of image, and potentially dangerous for its deceptive potential. According to Ricoeur, Aristotle sealed the destiny of metaphor "for centuries to come: henceforth it is connected to poetry and rhetoric, not at the level of discourse, but at the level of a segment of discourse, the name or noun"[12]. Metaphor's environment is defined as language, itself already ordered into genus and species and playing by already-determined rules. The rhetorical work of metaphor consists thus in the violation of this order and the rules of this game: to call the genus by the specie's name, and vice versa, means simultaneously recognizing and undermining the logical structure of language.

Cicero also viewed metaphor (*translatio*) as "a small similarity reduced into a single word"[13], whose function is essentially ornamental:

> There is a vast application for the use of metaphor: while arising out of necessity, from the poverty and limits of vocabulary, metaphor then acquired popularity for its pleasant character. Like clothes, which were invented to protect us from the cold but then began to be used to decorate the body, so also metaphor, created to compensate for the lack of words, came to be commonly used for pleasure.[14]

While classical rhetoric is interested in the displacement of meaning from the real to the figurative triggered by metaphor, the new rhetoric situates metaphor within a theory of argumentation. Reducing metaphor to a trope, Perelman defines it as "a condensed analogy, resulting from the fusion of an element of the *fora* with an element of the theme"[15]. Like Aristotle, Perelman considers metaphor to be a concentration of the analogical process: "any analogy—except those which present them-

---

[11] *Poetics*, III, 2, 1457b.
[12] P. Ricoeur, *The Rule of Metaphor*, London, 1977, p.14.
[13] Cicero, *De oratore*, III, p.39: "*Similitudinis est ad verbum unum contracta brevitas*".
[14] Ibid., III, p.38.
[15] C. Perelman and L. Olbrechts-Tyteca, *Trattato sull'argomentazione*, Turin, 1989, p.421.

selves in a rigid form, like allegory and parable—spontaneously becomes metaphor"[16]. Even in the new rhetoric metaphor remains an argumentative device[17].

III. The Semantic Paradigm of Metaphor

The rhetorical point of view gives way to the semantic one when "metaphor is transferred into the framework of the *sentence* and is treated not as a case of *deviant denomination*, but as a case of *impertinent predication*"[18]. An exclusively rhetorical conception of metaphor, whether classical or modern, depends upon the attribution of a privileged position to the word, to the name. A semantic analysis, by contrast, treats the phrase as the primary unit of meaning. Whereas rhetoric treats metaphor as a trope or a device which changes the meaning of a word through an analogy with another word, semantics regards metaphor as an unusual attribution at the level of the phrase or the discourse. A seminal work articulating the semantic conception of metaphor is Richards' *Philosophy of Rhetoric*. Richards conceives of rhetoric as a study of verbal understanding and misunderstandings. He thus begins his examination with a look at the dark side of communication, confusion, and then focuses on manipulation and language disturbances. For Richards, rhetoric becomes a study of verbal equivocations and their relative corrections. He declines to set forth a taxonomy, precisely because he aims to reassert the primacy of discourse over the word. For Richards, language is not just a system of signalling. And words are not tools for copying life, but for ordering it. Words are the places where experiences, which could never encounter each other at the level of feeling or intuition, somehow come together. They are the opportunity and the means for the mind's relentless attempt to order itself. Metaphor is not just another figure of speech, but an omnipresent principle of language. It is through metaphor that words, passing from one context to another,

---

[16] Ibid., p. 425.

[17] Cf. J. Derrida, *La mitologia bianca. La metafora nel testo filosofico*, in G. Conte (ed.), *Metafora*, Milan, 1981, p. 247: "Every time that rhetoric defines metaphor, this implies not only *a* philosophy but a conceptual web within which *the* philosophy is constituted. Moreover, every thread in this web forms a *turn of speech*, one could say a metaphor if this notion were not too derivative in this context. The defined is thus implied in the defining of the definition".

[18] Ricoeur, *The Rule of Metaphor*, p. 4.

change meaning. But there is no fixed, original, inherent meaning. The meaning of a word always depends upon the use that one makes of it and the purpose for which it is used. An exclusively rhetorical conception is insufficient, because metaphor must be situated within a process of interpretation. Richards thus puts forward a hermeneutical proposal:

> The theory of language may have something to learn, not much but a little, from the way in which the physicist envisages stabilities. But much closer analogies are possible with some of the patterns of Biology. The theory of interpretation is obviously a branch of biology—a branch that has not grown very far or very healthily yet. To remember this may help us to avoid some traditional mistakes—among them the use of bad analogies which tie us up if we take them too seriously. Some of these are notorious; for example, the opposition between form and content, and the almost equivalent opposition between matter and form. These are wretchedly inconvenient metaphors. So is that other which makes language a dress which thought puts on. We shall do better to think of a meaning as though it were a plant that has grown—not a can that has been filled or a lump of clay that has been moulded.[19]

While a theory of rhetoric is impossible, we can study the development of certain metaphors in order to understand the values that they further. A theory of metaphor is also impossible because every metaphor implies a comparison.

What is a comparison? It may be several different things: it may be just a putting together of two things to let them work together; it may be a study of them both to see how they are like and how unlike one another; or it may be a process of calling attention to their likenesses or a method of drawing attention to certain aspects of the one through the co-presence of the other. As we mean by comparison these different things we get different conceptions of metaphor.[20]

Thus Richards, in criticizing the sterility of a rhetorical and taxonomic approach, offers us a comparative vision of language and metaphor. Our way of perceiving and describing the function of a particular comparison/metaphor depends upon its purpose. While rhetoric views metaphor as a simple displacement of words, semantics views it instead as an exchange of thoughts, a transaction between contexts.

---

[19] Richards, *The Philosophy of Rhetoric*, p. 12.
[20] Ibid., p. 120.

As constitutive principles of language, the metaphors that we avoid shape our thought just as much as those we accept. The creation of metaphor is so marvelous and enigmatic that human attempts to describe and comprehend it are necessarily incomplete. But by observing the function of metaphor from the assumption of incomprehension, we can correct for the abuse of metaphor, by which it is used in order to conceal unspoken interests.

Our skill with metaphor, with thought, is one thing—prodigious and inexplicable; our reflective awareness of that skill is quite another thing—very incomplete, distorted, fallacious, over-simplifying. Its business is not to replace practice, or to tell us how to do what we cannot do already; but to protect our natural skill from the interferences of unnecessarily crude views about it; and, above all, to assist the imparting of that skill—that command of metaphor—from mind to mind. And progress here, in translating our skill into observation and theory, comes chiefly from profiting by our mistakes.[21]

Richards' insights were later taken up by Max Black. In his classic work, *Models and Metaphors*[22], Black articulates three conceptions of metaphor. First of all, there is the substitutive theory: in metaphor, one word substitutes another by virtue of its analogous meaning. According to the substitutive vision, metaphor is used to communicate a meaning that could have been expressed literally. If the writer substitutes L with M, the reader's job is to invert this substitution, using the literal meaning of L as a clue to understanding the literal meaning of M. Comprehending a metaphor is like decifering a code or solving a puzzle. Next, there is the comparative theory of metaphor, which is really a kind of substitution. This is an update of the Aristotelean vision of the metaphor as a condensed analogy （recall Quintilian, for whom "a simile is when I say that a man has behaved 'like a lion', a metaphor is when I say that a man 'is a lion'"[23]）. While the substitutive vision says that "Achilles is courageous", the comparative vision says that "Achilles is like a lion". One vision mentions courage, the other assumes it without saying so. Lastly, there is an interactive theory of metaphor: the reader or listener of a metaphorical expression is re-

---

[21] Ibid., p. 116.
[22] M. Black, *Modelli, archetipi, metafore*, Parma, 1992.
[23] Quintiliano, *Istituzione oratoria*, VIII, p. 6, p. 9.

quired to connect two ideas. Every metaphor contains two different ideas that act against each other, and meaning is the product of this interaction. If I say that the lion is the king of the jungle, I say both that the lion is on the highest level of a hierarchy, and also that monarchy is a necessary institution, even for animals (implying that animals are not capable of establishing a republic). The interactive theory imagines metaphor as a filter: the main subject is "seen through" the metaphorical expression; the image of Achilles is filtered through the icon of the lion. To call a man a lion means framing him in a special light, and also makes the lion seem more human!

Studying the metaphors, models and archetypes that structure scientific theories or legal doctrines does help us to appreciate the value of the imagination. But even if the rhetorical and semantic paradigms succeed in illuminating metaphor's function, they fail to say anything about the subject who is interpreting them. Neither rhetoric nor semantics widen the scope of the metaphorical field so far as to comprehend the fusion of horizons sought by the hermeneutical vision.

IV. The Structuralist Paradigm of Metaphor

But before examining the hermeneutical paradigm, we must consider the structuralist critique of metaphor. The structuralist attack is pointed: making metaphor the constitutive principle of language is both intellectually lazy, because it seeks to avoid the work of analyzing the differences between its tropes, as well as aphasic, because it ignores the parallel work of metonymy.

Taking up Richards' suggestion to study the pathological side of communication, Jakobson concentrated his attention on language disturbances. As the observation of children enables us to understand how language is acquired, so does the observation of aphasics enable us to understand how language is lost. Linguistics is interested in language in all of its aspects: language in practice, language in development, language being born, language in dissolution. Following Saussure, Jakobson observes how every linguistic sign implies two faculties: combination and selection. In *combination*, constitutive signs combine with each other and then with other signs; combination and contextualization are two aspects of the same process. In *selection*, alternative signs are chosen which can then substitute each other; selection and substitution are two aspects of the same process. While speaker has no freedom in the combination phase, because language is a predefined, indispensible, culturally-given code, there is more freedom in the selection phase, where it is possible to choose between multiple expressions. Observing aphasic disturbances, Jakobson notices that there can be two types of regression, which correspond to these two phases of language: a loss in the capacity of combination and a loss in the capacity of selection. Someone who loses the ability to contextualize mobilises only substitutive resources, and thus works only with similies, identifying things in a metaphorical way. Someone who loses the ability to select mobilises only contextualizing resources, and thus identifies things only in a metonymic way (for example, calling a telescope a microscope or a lantern fire).

The varieties of aphasia are numerous and diverse, but all of them lie between the two polar types just described. Every form of aphasic disturbance consists in some impairment, more or less severe, either of the faculty for selection and substitution or for combination and contexture. The former affliction involves a deterioration of metalinguistic operations, while the latter damages the capacity for maintaining the hierarchy of linguistic units. The relation of similarity is suppressed in the former, the relation of contiguity in the latter type of aphasia. Metaphor is alien to the similarity disorder, and metonymy to the contiguity disorder.[24]

Speech regression, like its development, unfolds along two different semantic axes, the metaphoric and metonymic. In the same way, we see that different historical epochs or cultural movements show a preference for metaphor or metonymy. In painting, it is clear how Cubism was inspired by a metonymic orientation, while surrealism preferred a metaphorical language. In film, Griffith favored a metonymic montage, varying the angle, the perspective and the center of the frame, while Chaplin preferred a metaphoric montage, introducing gradual dissolves. In literature, Romanticism favors metaphoric expressions, which Realism prefers metonymic ones.

Similarity in meaning connects the symbols of a metalanguage with the symbols of the language referred to. Similarity connects a metaphorical term with the term for which it is substituted. Consequently, when constructing a metalanguage to interpret

---

[24]   R. Jakobson and M. Halle, *Fundamentals of Language*, Paris, 1971, p. 90.

tropes, the researcher possesses more homogeneous means to handle metaphor, whereas metonymy, based on a different principle, easily defies interpretation. Therefore nothing comparable to the rich literature on metaphor can be cited for the theory of metonymy... Not only the tool of the observer but also the object of observation is responsible for the preponderance of metaphor over metonymy in scholarship. Since poetry is focused upon the sign, and pragmatical prose primarily upon the referent, tropes and figures were studied mainly as poetic devices... Thus, for poetry, metaphor, and for prose, metonymy is the line of least resistance and, consequently, the study of poetical tropes is directed chiefly toward metaphor. The actual bipolarity has been artificially replaced in these studies by an amputated, unipolar scheme which, strikingly enough, coincides with one of the two aphasic patterns, namely with the contiguity disorder.[25]

Gérard Genette shares Jakobson's idea that the preponderance of metaphor studies is due to a scientific afasia. He argues that privileging metaphor over metonymy implies a restriction of rhetoric. From the structuralist point of view, metaphor is only one form among many others, and its promotion to the status of analogy *par excellence* results from a kind of violence. Arguing against those who affirm that metaphor is the central figure of any rhetoric, Genette asserts that "thus, by virtue of an apparently universal and irrepressible centricism, the heart of rhetoric—or what is left of it—is no longer defined by the polar opposition between metaphor and metonymy, in which some air could still enter and some fragment of a great game could still circulate, but rather by the unadorned metaphor, frozen in its useless regality"[26]. The structuralist critique of the semantic approach to metaphor thus reduces metaphor to one trope among many. In this way, metaphor gets reabsorbed back into rhetoric.

An attempt to widen the horizons and functions of metaphor is put forward in the cognitivism of George Lakoff[27]. For Lakoff, metaphor permeates daily life, not only in language but also in thought and action. Examining ordinary language, we can locate some recurring metaphors. For example, expressions like "attack" a view, "defend" a thesis, argumentative "strategy", "gain" or "lose territory", suggest a

---

[25] Ibid., pp. 95—96.
[26] G. Genette, "La retorica ristretta", in G. Conte (ed.), *Metafora*, Milan, 1981, p. 220.
[27] G. Lakoff and M. Johnson, *Metaphors We Live By*, London, 1980.

common metaphorical reference to argumentation understood as war. Expressions such as "wasting" time playing, "gaining" time with a gadget, "investing" time in a study, "having" time at hand, suggest a common metaphorical reference to time understood as money. In the classic, *Metaphors We Live By*, Lakoff and Johnson present a metaphorical taxonomy, classifying the valences of metaphorical expressions. Arguing against objectivist conceptions, which presuppose a real meaning of words, Lakoff advances a constitutive vision of metaphor, which holds the meaning of words is produced.

Lakoff concentrates above all on the role of metaphor in political communication.[28] The art of framing, which means choosing the right slogan for introducing certain themes into the public debate, strongly conditions the substantive value of the matter in discussion. To speak about "abortion" is different from speaking about the "voluntary interruption of pregnancy", tilting us more in favor of the fetus's right to life than the mother's right to self-determination. Another example can be seen in the choice between "euthanasia" and "the right to death with dignity" (or "the right not to be subjected to aggressive therapy"): euthanasia accents the egoistic and hedonistic pleasure of the relativist who seeks escape from the inevitable suffering of life, while rights give value to the dignity of the autonomous decision to avoid useless, tragic suffering in the terminal phase of one's own existence.

Legal language provides cases of metaphorical transformations that reflect shifts in underlying political perceptions. An example from Italian law is the widespread practice of calling parliamentary laws by the name of their sponsors, which has the effect of reinforcing the personification of the political power and depriving the parliament as a whole of responsibility for its product. If the immigration law becomes the "Bossi-Fini", the immigration policies of the Italian state become the target of sympathies and antipathies towards two individual politicians, who in turn become the Italian state (a case of selective aphasia with a regression along the metonymic axis). Another example is the practice of calling some laws "arbitration", thus marking a public legislative act by a private law term; the law thus loses that civilizing veil of hypocrisy which portrayed it as an abstract provision aimed at protecting the general interest, to instead take on the brutal appearance of a private agreement aimed at

---

[28] Cf. G. Lakoff, *Don't Think of an Elephant!*, White River Junction, VT, 2004.

protecting the very particular interests of individuals. In calling a law an "arbitration", the politician who has rendered service to his boss gets linguistically promoted to the status of peace-maker who has successfully ended a conflict (a case of combinative aphasia, with a regression along the metaphorical axis).

Both the structuralist critique of metaphor and the cognitive revaluation of it shake up taxonomies in order to put metaphor in its proper place. While the structuralists reduce metaphor to a rhetorical figure, the cognitivists confine it at the center of language. While structuralism divides language into *langue* and *parole*, hermeneutics sees every speech act as an event. The truth of metaphors cannot emerge from the mechanical analogizing of the structuralist taxonomies, which reduce meaning to the identification and the reassignment of labels. Language is not just a code or a system, but a place in which human beings concentrate the meaning of their own experience.

V. The Hermeneutic Approach to Metaphor

Only with a hermeneutic approach can we hope to understand ourselves as standing before a world that reflects us, our prejudices and our convictions. The hermeneutics of metaphor requires not only an interpretation of the metaphor in light of the text, but also an interpretation of the text in light of the metaphor. Only in this way can the metaphoral word acquire meaning and value in a metaphorical discourse. Metaphor generates a fusion of horizons and an opening of the world, which tears the subject out of the self-referentiality of his own assumptions and traditional prejudices, requiring instead (and making possible) the imagination "no longer understood as the faculty of deriving 'images' from sensory experiences, but as the capacity to let new worlds construct our self-understanding. This power will not be given by new images, but by new meanings in our language. The imagination will then be regarded as a dimension of language. And a new relationship between imagination and metaphor will appear"[29]. Only a hermeneutic conception of metaphor places metaphor within the hermeneutic circle, which is not limited to figures of speech or structures of language, but embraces the horizons of received cultural traditions and the exis-

[29] P. Ricoeur, "Metafora e ermeneutica", in G. Conte (a cura di), *Metafora*, Milan, 1981, p. 170.

tential practices of a subject who interrogates a text by attributing meaning and value to it.

The pioneer of contemporary metaphor studies, Hans Blumenberg, synthesized both the semantic and structural conceptions of metaphor while, in a Hegelian fashion, he superceded them. While semantic views employed "paradigms" to focus on the mechanisms for displacing meaning, structural approaches studied the classifications of metaphor's persuasive and coercive effects. For Blumenberg, by contrast, only a hermeneutic conception could do justice to the value of metaphor: a metaphor is not just an enunciation that can be reduced into concepts, nor a disciplinary strategy making use of manipulative rhetorics to subordinate individuals, but rather a point of condensation for historically-conditioned cultures and traditions. So, for example, European metaphors are more organic, while American metaphors are more mechanistic. The rhetorical origin of metaphor corresponds to its original ambiguity: "metaphor undoubtedly has its roots in the ambivalence of ancient rhetoric: the orator can let the truth 'appear' in its legitimate splendor, but can also make the false assume the same appearance as the truth"[30].

The "literal meaning" is in fact the flood lands formed by the disaggregation and commingling of the old metaphorical rocks. According to Blumenberg, there are thus some archetypal metaphors, continually invoked in order to designate phenomena for which there is no specific figure and that cannot therefore be reduced to conceptual terms (such as law, the force of law, constitution, state, sovereignty). From the hermeneutical standpoint, metaphor's value is not objective and intrinsic, but rather depends on the context in which it is inserted and on the tradition from which it emanates.

In his masterpiece, *The Rule of Metaphor*, Ricoeur argues for a hermeneutical conception: "metaphor presents itself as a strategy of discourse that, while preserving and developing the creative power of language, preserves and develops the *heuristic* power wielded by fiction".[31] "Through metaphor, subjectivity opens up to the tension of the truth, required by the fictitious aspect of the category or the concept. This is obviously a metaphorical, comparative truth, which interrogates the meaning

---

[30] H. Blumenberg, *Paradigmi per una metaforologia*, Bologna, 1969, p. 114.
[31] Ricoeur, "Metafora e ermeneutica", p. 6.

of translation".[32]

In the great majority of studies dedicated to metaphor, be they rhetorical or semantic, we do not see a due respect paid to the insuperable contribution of Nietzsche's early essay on truth and lying. A master of metaphor, Nietzsche reflects on the birth and development of language in the phase of his own life in which he left philology to pursue the fusion of poetry and philosophy that would mark his unmistakable style. Nietzsche imagines a scene very much like the beginning of *2001: A Space Odyssey*: "in some remote corner of the universe, poured out and glittering in innumerable solar systems, there once was a star on which clever animals invented knowledge"[33]. This fable imagines that the invention of language corresponds to the original sin of the claim to truth: the word is the result of three metaphorical leaps of translation: a nerve stimulus is translated into an image, an image into a sound, a sound into a word. Words cannot correspond to things, because they are the product of these leaps in the sensory realm. Even when comparing words in different languages that are supposed to mean the same thing, we come up against the ultimate impossibility of translation, and must disabuse ourselves of the false pretense of actually grasping the noumenous, ontological essence of things:

> The different languages, set side by side, show that what matters with words is never the truth, never an adequate expression; else there would not be so many languages. The "thing in itself" (for that is what pure truth, without consequences, would be) is quite incomprehensible to the creators of language and is not at all worth aiming for. One designates only the relations of things to man, and to express them one calls on the boldest metaphors. A nerve stimulus, first transposed into an image—first metaphor. The image, in turn, imitated by a sound—second metaphor. And each time there is a complete overleaping of one sphere, right into the middle of an entirely new and different one.[34]

Nietzsche is not simply making the nihilistic argument that there is no truth. In

---

[32] Ibid., p.152.

[33] F. Nietzsche, "On Truth and Lie in an Extra-Moral Sense", from the Nachlass. Compiled from translations by Walter Kaufmann and Daniel Breazeale. http://www.geocities.com/thenietzschechannel/tls.htm.

[34] Ibid.

emphasizing the importance of translation in the transformation of sounds into images and then into words, Nietzsche advances the paradoxical idea that the very "nature" of truth claims is metaphorical, that there is only metaphorical truth:

> What, then, is truth? A mobile army of metaphors, metonyms, and anthropomorphisms—in short, a sum of human relations, which have been enhanced, transposed, and embellished poetically and rhetorically, and which after long use seem firm, canonical, and obligatory to a people: truths are illusions about which one has forgotten that this is what they are; metaphors which are worn out and without sensuous power; coins which have lost their pictures and now matter only as metal, no longer as coins.[35]

While metaphorical creativity is the pulse of life, the conceptual order is created and imposed by subjects incapable of abandoning themselves to artistic, mythological or onirical ecstasy. The metaphorical style is a sign of the fullness of life, just as the "demonstrative" style suggests its impoverishment. Nietzsche lavishes particular scorn upon those those who (like myself) make a profession out of scientific research, for having fled from metaphorical heights to seek refuge in dead concepts:

> We have seen how it is originally *language* which works on the construction of concepts, a labor taken over in later ages by *science*. Just as the bee simultaneously constructs cells and fills them with honey, so science works unceasingly on this great columbarium of concepts, the graveyard of perceptions. It is always building new, higher stories and shoring up, cleaning, and renovating the old cells; above all, it takes pains to fill up this monstrously towering framework and to arrange therein the entire empirical world, which is to say, the anthropomorphic world. Whereas the man of action binds his life to reason and its concepts so that he will not be swept away and lost, the scientific investigator builds his hut right next to the tower of science so that he will be able to work on it and to find shelter for himself beneath those bulwarks which presently exist. And he requires shelter, for there are frightful powers which continuously break in upon him, powers which oppose scientific truth with completely different kinds of "truths" which bear on their shields the most varied sorts of emblems.[36]

---

[35] Ibid.
[36] Ibid.

For Nietzsche, therefore, every metaphor is intuitive and singular and incommensurable, thus eluding any classification. Notwithstanding this, because the genial creator of metaphors does not learn from his own experience, reason seeks incessantly to reify metaphorical life in conceptual abstractions. Doing this, the rational mind imagines an ontological substance lying behind a nominalistic appearance and seeks refuge in a conceptual order, presented as objective, neutral or natural, but which is really arbitrary, value-laden and partial. A theory of metaphor is impossible because it reduces metaphor to theory when its very nature is metaphorical.

What then is the point of speaking around, through or by means of metaphors? According to Nietzsche, "the new philosopher does not use metaphors in the rhetorical sense, but rather subordinates them to a correct language or a strategic aim: he uses non-stereotypical metaphors in order to reveal the deeper metaphors that constitute every concept"[37]. It is in this way that the hermeneutics approach to metaphor has a meaning for the law: the goal of legal analysis is to become aware of the metaphorical nature of normative language, to show the values contained and furthered by legal metaphors and to call attention to the abuse of metaphor committed by apparently neutral and impartial concepts.

While rhetoric, semantics and structuralism do not consider the historical embodiment of the interpreting subject, hermeneutics regards the individual's being in time and his critical evocation of his own traditions as necessarily creative of meaning. For a hermeneutical approach, the classification of legal metaphors can serve as a first step in a serious study of them. But the ultimate goal is to narrate the genealogies of legal metaphors and critically analyze the values that they serve. The genealogical reconstruction of a metaphor is not itself sufficient because "hardening and congealing of a metaphor guarantees absolutely nothing concerning its necessity and exclusive justification".[38] So, in the face of historically embedded metaphors, we come back to considerations of the uses and disadvantages of metaphor for life.[39] If the legal scholar is active and ambitious, he will tend to construct a monumental his-

---

[37] Cf. S. Kofman, *Nietzsche et la métaphore*, Paris, 1972, p. 31.

[38] F. Nietzsche, "On Truth and Lie in an Extra-Moral Sense".

[39] F. Nietzsche, "On the Uses and Disadvantages of History for Life", in *Untimely Meditations* (R. J. Hollingdale, trans.), Cambridge, 1983.

toricity; if he seeks to preserve and revere, he will tend to construct an antiquated historicity; if he suffers and seeks liberation, he will tend to construct a critical historicity. A critical hermeneutic of metaphor examines the history of legal doctrines, without instrumentalizing them to serve a contemporary debate nor venerating them for a glorious future. It renounces the aspiration of explaining how law is created and how it functions, in order to focus on metaphorical expressions' potential for distortion and abuse.

I would like to conclude with the important admonition of Richards:

> It is an old dream that in time psychology might be able to tell us so much about our minds that we would at last become able to discover with some certainty what we mean by our words and how we mean it. An opposite or complementary dream is that with enough improvement in Rhetoric we may in time learn so much about words that they will tell us how our minds work. It seems modest and reasonable to combine these dreams and hope that a patient persistence with the problems of Rhetoric may, while exposing the causes and modes of the misinterpretation of words, also throw light upon and suggest a remedial discipline for deeper and more grievous disorders.[40]

---

[40] Richards, *The Philosophy of Rhetoric*, p. 136.

The Role of Equity in Judicial Discretion in Turkish Law and the Perception of Equity of Turkish Judges

Eylem Ümit Atilgan

I. Introduction

This paper is a theoretical evaluation of the data obtained from a field survey of judges and public prosecutors. During the in-depth interviews I held with the most capable and experienced judges in the Turkish judiciary system, as well as with public prosecutors, I attempted to understand what judges mean by the concept of equity and the way they apply it when delivering a verdict. In this respect, the study is an attempt at the field of activity which Dworkin refers to "as answering the question of what law is from the judge's perspective".[1] According to Volkmar Gessner's demonstration of framework to the legal culture research, courts are one of the institutional actors and they build up the field three which is called comparative implementation research. Following Professor Gessner's definition of legal culture, it can be said

---

[1] Michael S. Moore, "Legal Principles Revisited", *Lowa L. Review*, V. 82, 1997, pp. 867—891.

that, this study involves with a components of legal cultures by focusing on the judges perceptions.[2]

The information I will present here is actually the broad conclusions from the data I obtained at the first stage of a long and comprehensive study. What establishes the framework of the study is the question of "how judges make decisions". In seeking an answer to this question, I have so far conducted in-depth interviews with about 80 judges.[3] At the next stage, I plan to hold interviews at the high courts level. Since I designed the research in accordance with a qualitative method, its pur-

---

[2] Volkmar Gessner, "On the Methodology of Comparing Legal Phenomena" in Volkmar Gessner, Armin Hoeland, Csaba Varga eds., *European Legal Cultures*, Dartmouth, 1996, p. 245; Ali Acar, "The Concept of Legal Culture, With Particular Attention to the Turkish Case", *Ankara Law Review*, Vol. 3, No. 2, winter 2006, p. 150.

[3] The questionnaire of the semi structured depth-interviews is as follows:

Q1st What are the resources which you apply most, regarding your profession? Among those resources, what is the place of the case law (the decisions of the court of appeals) and how often the case law is applied? What can you say about the role of case law in judicial process considering your observations on your colleagues?

Q2nd In your view, how should the statement "the code shall be applied on the subjects where it refers literally and substantially" be interpreted?

Q3rd (To judges of civil courts) Do you meet with the legal gaps too often? What is the way that should be followed by judges when a legal gap is met in the proceedings?

Q4th What are the instruments which are used by the judges applying the judicial discretion? What instruments should be used by the judges applying the judicial discretion?

Q5th What are the borders of the judicial discretion? What should they be?

Q6th How should a judge act in cases where he does not find the norms that must be applied appropriate?

Q7th Please mark the expressions which you find appropriate below
- Personal conditions should be considered in proceedings.
- The environment where the event which caused the trial occurred should be considered in the proceedings.
- Both personal and environmental conditions should be considered in the proceedings.
- Personal and environmental conditions should be ignored and the law should be applied to everyone objectively.

Q8th What is the role of the equity in the judicial process?

Q9th What does equitable judgment mean in your point of view?

Q10th (To judges of criminal courts) In your view, what is the role of discretional extenuation governed under Article 62 of Turkish Penal Code (which is also called "extenuation of necktie" in public speech in Turkey) in judicial activity? How is it applied in practice and how should it be applied? (What is your opinion about orientation, social conditions and to be damaged because of the crime?

Q11th What is your opinion on the results relating the personal conviction of the judges in legislating techniques? How do you define personal conviction? (Article 138 (1) of Turkish Constitution: "Judges shall be independent in the discharge of their duties; they shall give judgment in accordance with the Constitution, law, and their personal conviction conforming with the law")

pose is to understand rather than survey and assess. Thus, quality is the priority in the data, as opposed to quantity in a quantitative study. I should also note that the data I have so far obtained exceeds a duration of 90 hours. The information I will share with you here consists of a preliminary analysis of the data and the basic conclusions I obtained. It goes without saying that the new contexts to be drawn from the second analysis will enrich and deepen these conclusions.

Ⅱ. The Concept of Equity

As a preliminary remark, I have to stress that concept of equity is never univocal in Turkish jurisprudence. Actually, equity (aequitas-equité-billigkeit) is a term which has different meanings in comparative law too. In the English legal tradition, the term technically means a part of English law originally administrated by the Lord Chancellor and later by the Court of Chancery as distinct from that administrated by the courts of common law. These courts were later to be called the "courts of equity".[4] Law of equity was developed separately from the body of law as laid down by the common law courts from about the 15th century.[5] The rules, maxims and practice of equity were shaped during the equity jurisdiction.[6]

On the other hand, although the continental codes (like the French, German, Swiss civil codes) contain many references to it, equity is not defined in any of these codes.[7] But it is obvious that in the continental judicial tradition, equity plays a significant role in adapting the written law to the rapidly changing society through the concepts of interpretation and the judges' powers of discretion. As it is always said by continental jurists: "Summum jus summa injura" ("The rigor of the law is the height of oppression")—here there is no doubt that equity leaves the code vague for

---

Q12th　(To judges of Criminal Courts) (Article 217 of Criminal Procedure Code: Estimation of Evidence—Judge may rely on only the evidences which were brought and discussed in the hearings. Those evidences shall be estimated by personal conviction of the judge without constraint.)

　　Q13.

　[4]　Also Called Courts of Conscience.

　[5]　Harold Greville Hanbury, *Modern Equity, The Principles of Equity*, seventh edition, London, 1957, pp. 1—9; G. W. Keeton, *An Introduction to Equity*, London, 1938, pp. 1—39.

　[6]　Keeton, *An Introduction to Equity*, pp. 104—107.

　[7]　Peter De Cruz, *Comparative Law in a Changing World*, 2nd edition, Routledge, 1999, p. 216.

judicial interpretation and judicial interpretation allows the law to evolve with society.[8]

True, the origin of the common law and civil law systems' concepts of equity are only roughly the same.[9] True English equity, developed from the intersection of Greek, Roman and Christian traditions, represented the perfect and powerful incarnation of the paradigm of political theology. In fact, in spite of the etymology, the concept of equity (English equity) is a translation of the Greek idea of epieikeia much more than of the Latin aequitas, so the set of associations of different, linguistic and conceptual elements reintroduces the issue of the roots of Western tradition when it ends up as equity in English.[10]

There is no doubt that the concept of equity in the Continental law tradition is more directly related to the Roman aequitas than the English equity.

The word aequitas, the equivalent of the English term "equity" in Roman law, was defined as "related to justice but distinguished from the positive law (ius)" in dictionaries of Roman law. Indeed, an examination into its historical use demonstrates that ius and aequitas have often been so closely related that they have become inseparable.

The concept was used at times as opposite to "the written law (ius)" and served a corrective function for the current law. Looking back to definitions again, one of these defines the term as "one of the main principles which guide or are supposed to guide the development of law", while another one states that "it is one of the corrective and creative elements in the development of law". Aequitas is observed either in interpreting the written law or filling the gaps in a statute. In this context, we should also note that many jurists of Roman law underline the relationship between natural law and equity.

As a matter of fact, we see prominent jurists endorsing and celebrating the rejection of the Roman-scholastic notion of law during the period when equity was in-

---

[8] To point out this mission of judges, they are called "living codes" by some legal scholars. Faruk Erem, *Psychology of Justice*, 8th edition, Ankara, 1988, p. 321.

[9] Charles S. Brice, "Roman Aequitas and English Equity", *Georgetown Law Journal*, V. 2, 1913—1914, pp. 16—24.

[10] Cristina Constantini, *Equity Different Talks*, Social Science Research Network, Working Paper Series, 2008, pp. 3—6; Alastair Hudson, *Equity & Trust*, Routledge, 2003, p. 8.

troduced into modern laws as a principle, that is, when Article 1 of the Swiss Civil Code was discussed and embraced. While the meaning of this first article was under discussion, a phrase which was included in the draft of the French Civil Law and was referred to by the jurists of the time is important in that it articulates the relationship between equity and natural law: "there exists an unchanging and universal law as the source of positive laws (lois positives), which is nothing but the natural reason governing men."[11]

III. The Concept of Equity And Judicial Discretion in Turkish Law

Turkey adopted the Swiss Civil Code, which clearly charges judges with the task of deciding and exercising their powers of discretion in accordance with equity.[12] Concerning the motives behind this choice in the Swiss Civil Code, which underlined the role of judges in the sources and implementation of law, Professor Eugen Huber, the writer of the preliminary draft, stated in his report as follows:

> We do not believe it would be advantageous if the legislature deprived the courts of all discretion in recognizing this point. The interpretation may vary, during the existence of the statute, in accordance with the opportunities of the text and the state of public conscience, and it would be a mistake to draw a statute in such a way as to make it impossible for the courts to follow the development of public opinion without a change of the text.... When the legislator intends to make a provision absolutely mandato-

---

[11] Claude du Pasquier, "New Ideas in Appliance of the Law and the Court Decisions", *Ankara University Law Faculty Review*, translated by Jale Akipek, V.11, No.3—4, 1954, pp.310—311.

[12] Related articles in Turkish Civil Codes are as follows:

"A. Sources and Enactment of Law

Art 1

The written law is applicable to all matters to which either the letter or spirit of any of its provisions refer. In the absence of a provision of such law applicable to a case, the judge shall decide according to customary law and in the absence of custom, according to the rule which he would establish were he acting as legislator. He shall base his decisions upon the solutions adopted by doctrine (writers) and in judicial decisions."

III. Judicial Power of Discretion

Art 4

The judge shall decide in accordance with law and equity in matters where the law grants the power of discretion or prescribes the consideration of the needs of a situation or justified reasons.

ry, he should say so. Where he fails to say so, the question will be decided in accordance with the spirit of the times.[13]

Apart from the Preliminary Provisions of the Turkish Civil Code, which were legislated in the same manner as the Swiss Civil Code, the legislator refers the concept of equity in various codes, including phrases such as "equitable compensation", "shall decide in accordance with equity". Furthermore, we should note that the concept of "conscientious conviction", a term closely related to equity, and the principle of rendering a verdict in accordance with conscientious conviction are both constitutional guarantees.[14] As a matter of fact, an examination of the codes reveals that equity is among the general standards of law, just like concepts such as "a reasonable period of time", "critical reasons", "special conditions", "the offender's past and social relations, the offender's behaviors following the perpetration of a crime and during the judicial process, consequences of the penalty for the future of the offender", and constitutes one of the sources of legal uncertainty as noted by Hart.[15] In order to consider the role of the principle of equity in judicial activity from a broader perspective, we will take a brief look into the judicial procedures currently in force in Turkey:

During the beginning of a particular case, i. e. the first stage of the judicial activity, the judge is supposed to obtain as clear a picture as possible of the case before him/her. In answering the questions of whether the incident really took place, and where, how and when it took place if it did, the judge uses an inductive method.

---

[13] Francois Geny, "The Legislative Technique of Modern Civil Codes", in *Science of Legal Method*: *Selected Essays*, *Modern Legal Philosophy*, V. 9, Chapter XII, sec. 13, Ernest Bruncken ed., Boston, 1917.

[14] The article of the constitution is as follows

Art 138

Independence of the Courts

Judges shall be independent in the discharge of their duties; they shall give judgments in accordance with the Constitution, law, and their personal conviction (conscience) conforming with the law. No organ, authority, office or individual may give orders or instructions to courts or judges relating to the exercise of judicial power, send them circulars, or make recommendations or suggestions.

No questions shall be asked, debates held, or statements made in the Legislative Assembly relating to the exercise of judicial power concerning a case under trial. Legislative and executive organs and the administration shall comply with court decisions; these organs and the administration shall neither alter them in any respect, nor delay their execution.

[15] M. D. A. Freeman, *Introduction to Jurisprudence*, Sweet-Maxwell, 1994, pp. 1269—1271.

This stage is actually a sort of assessment activity where the judge authenticates the case. At this stage, the judge is not in the world of law, but rather identifies the case by means of the inductive method and using the impression and information s/he obtains through the five senses in the physical and psychological world (such as finding during the investigation that the food stuff is rotten), the rules of experience (such as the impossibility, under normal conditions, of recalling with all its details an event which happened a long time ago) and technical information (such as referring to a forensic expert for the time of the crime of murder).

The long-dated books I read for this stage used the title "hakîm" meaning "eminently prudent and erudite in all matters, philosopher", which is one of the definitions of the judge in the Mecelle [the Compendium]. A judge makes assessment and arrives at a decision both at this first stage and the second stage, which consists of legal denomination, i. e. finding the legal norm appropriate for a particular event and situation, and is also called legal description, denomination, argumentation or legal rhetoric. Given that assessment of evidence takes place at this stage, we can once more conclude that the obligation for the judge to decide in accordance with law and equity applies to this stage as well.

Indeed, the role of equity should not be simply confined to Article 4 of the Turkish Civil Code, because treating equity without detaching it from justice (which should actually be the case), makes it a superior principle of the system.

Doctrinally, the principles are listed according to their varying meanings on the basis of the contexts in which they are used, and there is reference to five categories of principles:

(1) A principle which refers to a general norm: It refers to a principle of a general nature in terms of its scope, such as the norm which is applicable to contracts of every kind.

(2) A principle which refers to a norm constructed using ambiguous terms: Here, there is the use of ambiguous and ambivalent concepts and terms, such as the abuse of a right or goodwill.

(3) A principle which refers to a norm describing a legal system, one of its elements and the paramount values of one of its institutions, such as the principle of justice as the most supreme value and the principle of equity in terms of its relationship to justice.

(4) A principle which refers to a norm stipulating an obligation in order to achieve a certain policy or an end, such as ensuring the protection of customers by the authorities through effective measures.

(5) A principle pertaining to the bodies exercising law, such as the principle specifying the method of selecting the norm to be applied, or systematizing the law.[16]

So, what does equity encompass as a principle?

In his work The Rhetoric, Aristotle establishes the following relationship between equity, mercy and a person's story, intention, and personal situation:

> Equity bids us be merciful to the weakness of human nature; to think less about the laws than about the man who framed them, and less about what he said than about what he meant; not to consider the actions of the accused so much as his intentions, nor this or that detail so much as the whole story; to ask not what a man is now but what he has always or usually been. It bids us remember benefits rather than injuries, and benefits received rather than benefits conferred; to be patient when we are wronged; to settle a dispute by negotiation and not by force; to prefer arbitration to motion-for an arbitrator goes by the equity of a case, a judge by the strict law, and arbitration was invented with the express purpose of securing full power for equity. The above may be taken as a sufficient account of the nature of equity.[17]

In his work titled Nicomachean Ethics, Aristotle underlines the role of equity in applying justice as a more abstract and general principle to a particular case.

> What creates the problem is that the equitable is just, but not the legally just but a correction of legal justice. The reason is that all law is universal but about some things it is not possible to make a universal statement which shall be correct. In those cases, then, in which it is necessary to speak universally, but not possible to do so correctly, the law takes the usual case, though it is not ignorant of the possibility of error. And it is none the less correct, for the error is in the law nor in the legislator but in the nature of the thing, since the matter of practical affairs is of this kind from the start. When the law speaks universally, then, and a case arises on it which is not covered by the universal statement, then it is right, where the

---

[16] Gülriz Uygur, *Law, Ethics and Principles*, 2006, pp. 13—14.
[17] Aristotle, *Rethorik*, pp. 84—85.

legislator fails us and has erred by oversimplicity, to correct the omission-to say what the legislator himself would have said had he been present, and would have put into his law if he had known. Hence the equitable is just, and better than one kind of justice-not better than absolute justice but better than the error that arises from the absoluteness of the statement. And this is the nature of the equitable, a correction of law where it is defective owing to its universality. In fact this is the reason why all things are not determined by law, that about some things it is impossible to lay down a law, so that a decree is needed. For when the thing is indefinite the rule also is indefinite.[18]

As is clear from the quotes by Aristotle, equity and justice are intertwined. When filling the gaps and considering the changing conditions, equity greatly contributes to justice, whereas in stipulating uneven procedures for uneven conditions, it once more and indirectly ensures the administration of justice although, at first glance, it appears to violate equality.[19]

The similar and different terms corresponding to equity in Roman Law could be listed as follows: "justice in a particular case", "equitable/conscientious", "correction of the notion of justice emanating from the law", "same treatment for the same event", or "acting in accordance with equality, expediency".[20]

Besides Aristotle, the works of Cicero constitute another important source on the uses of equity. Transposing to a great extent Aristotle's thoughts into Roman Law, Cicero makes a crucial comment on equity: "The greatest justice can be the greatest injustice; that is, the stricter is the application of a legal rule to a particular case, the more unjust, or inequitable, are its consequences. Summum ius summa iniuira."[21]

Almost all texts about equity define the two basic interrelated functions of the concept in question: the function of equity pertaining to justice serves to arrive at a fair conclusion by administering justice, an abstract and general principle, to a particular case. The term "justice in a particular case" is referred to as corresponding to

---

[18] Aristotle, *Nicomachean Ethics*, p.14.
[19] Kadir Gürten, *Aequitas In Roman Law*, 2008, p.32. Edward Roelker, "The Meaning of Aequitas, Aequus and Aeque In the Code of Canon", in *The Jurist*, V.6, 1946, pp.239—274.
[20] Gürten, ibid., p.48.
[21] Gürten, ibid., p.59.

this very function. In all decisions the judge makes by considering the requirements of a particular case, there is a reference to the judge's obligation to make an equitable decision in this respect.[22]

Hegel set out the following definition of equity underlying the function of "the justice in particular case":

> Equity involves a departure from formal rights owing to moral or other considerations and is concerned primarily with the content of law suit. A court of equity, however, comes to mean a court which decides in a single case without insisting formalities of a legal process or in particular, on the objective evidence which the letter of the law may require. Further, it decides on the merits of the single case as a unique one, not with a view to disposing of it in such a way to create a binding legal precedent or future.[23]

On the other hand, the second function is closely related to the first and refers to the relaxation of the law so as to prevent possible injustices brought by the strict application of the law. Historical process demonstrates that British Equity Courts contribute to the development of the law of equity by performing this function. It is obvious that this second function of equity relates to its corrective and constructive role in the development of law, as stated by Aristotle and Cicero. As noted in the recognized definitions of equity which I quoted at the beginning of this presentation, the decisive role of equity in the development of law is considered either in interpreting the current law or filling the gaps in a statute.

IV. The Perceptions of Equity of Turkish Judges

In this conceptual framework where I confined myself rather to a brief glance into remarks on the meaning and the role of the concept equity, I also would like to focus on the functions of equity in intertwined areas. The corrective and creative role of equity in the development of law, which we referred to as its second function, manifests itself in the fields of interpretation and filling gaps. To begin with the question

---

[22] Court of Appeals (Yargitay) clearly defines equity as "justice in particular case" in several decisions. For instance 9. H. D. 1968, E. 691, K. 4629; 2. H. D. E. 2006/12234, K. 2006/18458, T. 27. 12. 2006; 2. H. D. E. 2007/539, K. 2007/16529, T. 27. 11. 2007.

[23] G. W. F. Hegel, *Philosophy of Right*, 1821, translated by T. M. Knox, 1952, paragraph 223.

of interpretation, by stipulating in Art 1 that "The written law is applicable to all matters to which either the letter or spirit of any of its provisions refer". Article 1 of the Turkish Civil Code refers to the activity of applying abstract rules to concrete cases through methods of interpretation such as literal, teleological, historical and systematic interpretation. Leaving outside the scope of the present text the data on how Turkish judges resort to which interpretation method and what the most frequently used method is, I would like to emphasize the general approach of our judges towards interpretation. With its function of justice in a particular case, interpretation is of particular importance for the principle of equity.

Let us briefly examine of the perception of interpretation involved in two different approaches. We already know that by stripping the judge off the task of seeking and ascertaining the will of the legislator and even going beyond, the sociological approach defines law as what the courts will do. In its purest form, legal positivism has a formalist understanding of interpretation, while legal realism's understanding of interpretation is teleological interpretation.

In the formalist understanding, the interpreter asks himself/herself the following question: How should I interpret the written rule before me in order to comply with the will of its legislator? In the sociological approach, the interpreter, on the contrary, deals with how the law should be administered and shaped in order to achieve the aims of meeting the needs of social life awaiting satisfaction and restoring the disturbed balances which need to be reestablished.

In their responses to the question about interpretation, the term I most frequently heard from our judges was the Court of Appeals (Turkish name—Yargitay). Most judges, so to speak, changed the question posed by an interpreter in the formalist interpretation to "How should I interpret the rule before me so that I comply with the will of the Court of Appeals?" The dominant role of the Court of Appeals come into prominence regarding the face-to-face, open court and direct judicial hearings which are essential to understand what the "justice in particular case" is. I would like to quote some brief examples from the interviews. As the original words of judges and public prosecutors, they are very striking:

> Judge: "(...) so what does the Court of Appeals want?" It is far beyond the spirit and letter of the law; first of all, I think that judges are definitely

and excessively constrained by the question about "What does the Court of Appeals think about it?"—which prevents them from thinking what is beyond.

Another interviewee used exactly the following phrase about the issue of interpretation:

> Judge: Administration is literal in our country.
> EÜ: What about the spirit of the law?
> Judge: Of course you are bound by the Court of Appeals for it has the last word. We have to act as the Court of Appeals says. Otherwise, if we act in accordance with the spirit of the law, our spirits will be ruined.

What the interviewee refers to by saying "our spirits will be ruined" is the grading system required for promotion.[24] Below is another interviewee's interpretation of the effect of grading and promotion system upon legal proceedings:

> Judge: We look at the jurisprudence to see how the Court of Appeals decided on a matter. Because the Court of Appeals is the authority to make the final judgment, and to reverse a judgment to send it back to us ... it might impede or adversely affect our promotion. Even if we resist, the case will be referred to the General Board of Criminal Department, whose opinions are based on certain jurisprudence; therefore, I am against the practice of grading in the Court of Appeals. Yet, it is our job anyway and completely automatic promotions are wrong. They could introduce a different promotion system so as to ensure greater attention. They could introduce another promotion system that particularly serves autonomy. Yet, the grading system really affects the conscientious convictions of judges.

The interviewees continued to comment on their experiences and observations on the issue:

> Judge: I have always observed that many judges do not seek to discover the truth, they rather "seek to make irreversible decisions". I have even seen some colleagues who first shaped the case in their minds before listening to the witnesses, and asked the questions accordingly.

---

[24] The consequences of the grading system of The Court of Appeal have been discussed by jurists for a long time in Turkey. Some judges name this system as "supreme court oligarchy". See Kemal Şahin (Judge of Kazan), "Division of Powers and The Judicial Independency in Turkey", in: *Arkiv For Philosophy and Sociology of Law HFSA*, V. 16, 2007, p. 237.

E Ü: So they resort to jurisprudence even in the case assessment stage, don't they?

An interviewee evaluates the shadow of the Court of Appeals in interpretation with its very role in the doctrine:

Judge: I mean the laws are increasingly deprived of their spirit. Why? For we are jurists, but we, most of us, gave up on our powers to become technicians. Thus, the spirit is lost but in general we are good at literal interpretation, for there are others who show us how to. We have masters before us. We literally implement the laws but they have no spirit. Why? Because teleological interpretation is missing. Unless we make teleological interpretations, we only have an article of law before us, which we should use and apply in any conflict. We are content by simply saying "we cannot act otherwise; this is the task of legislation". If the law is wrong, legal arrangements will be made, legislation performs its duty and will abolish or amend the article, only after which I can change its administration. If you say so, then you will be interpreting the law literally. But you will never be making teleological interpretations; justice in particular case will never manifest itself; and you will never decide in accordance with equity. This is what I think.

I found that a minority of the judges who complained of the present situation recommended the teleological interpretation for the interpretational approach, which should be more often used in practice. Nevertheless, what is particularly underlined in the sociological approach to law for teleological interpretation is that judges should make use of, and be learned in, social sciences such as sociology, philosophy and psychology. My impression about the interviews is that the lack of information in these fields has been compensated for with a "knowledge of life". I regret to say that I very often observed subjective evaluations and prejudices about the regular course of life. The judges told me that they often made use of prejudices concerning ethnic, religious and sexual attributes as knowledge of life, and thus, they accordingly administered justice in particular case. These subjective evaluations and prejudices remind me "subconscious element in the judicial process" definition of Cardozo. He says "it is often through these subconscious forces that judges kept consistent with themselves and inconsistent with one another". [25] Cardozo implies that it is not easy for a judge to be aware of subconscious forces:

> All their lives, which they do not recognize and cannot name, have been tugging at them—inherited instincts, traditional beliefs, acquired convictions; and the resultant is an outlook on life, a conception of social needs (...)[26]

During the interviews I usually observed that some of judges name "knowledge of life" or "justice in particular case" to the subconscious elements and cover them.[27] To provide a few examples from the interviews:

> > A woman appears and says "this man harassed me". I look at them and see the husband is ugly but the other man is handsome. Then I conclude that the woman wanted to have an affair with this man, but then she yielded to social pressure and claimed that it was harassment to save face.
>
> > They brought the man before me for smuggling. The guy is from Kilis[28], he must have absolutely done it.
>
> > We have become judges of character. When I look at a man's face, it is clear to me whether he is the perpetrator.

With my colleagues with whom I shared such examples, of which I have quoted only a few, we thought that this phenomenon reminded us of a qadi's activity. Actually as it is rightly said by Gadamer, "It is not so much our judgments as it is our prejudices that constitute our being".[29] He restores to its rightful place a positive concept of prejudice and implies prejudices are not necessarily unjustified and erroneous, so that they inevitably distort the truth. Prejudices are simply conditions

---

[25] Benjamin Nathan Cardozo, *The Nature of the Judicial Process* (originally published in 1921), 2009, p. 12.

[26] loc. cit.

[27] A former judge Professor Dinçkol states that, wrong judgments of the judges are mostly caused by prejudices. Especially performing profession for long time could engrave the prejudices. And those prejudices interfere in the judicial process unconsciously. Judge should be awake and a hard worker to avoid from this situation. Abdullah Dinçkol, "Basic Principals of Judicial Judgment Process", in: *Arkiv For Philosophy and Sociology of Law*, V. 2, 1995, p. 175.

[28] A border town.

[29] Hans-Georg Gadamer, *Philosophical Hermeneutics*, 2nd Edition, David E. Linge trans. & ed., 2008, p. 9.

whereby we experience something and they are biases of our openness to the world.[30] The essential and vital issue about prejudices is not about "having or not having them", but hiding them. So taking off the curtains covering them is necessary to ascertain. Gadamer defines "knowing how to distinguish between blind prejudices and those which illuminate, between false prejudices and true prejudices" as the critical task of hermeneutics.[31]

Since this study is first and foremost based on a qualitative field survey, I should particularly avoid generalizations and jump into definitive conclusions. However, it would not be wrong to argue that judging the case from the available picture is open to the impact of value judgments. At this juncture, I believe the distinction between morality and ethics gains prominence. As is well known, morality is defined as the systems of value judgments concerning behaviors prevailing in a certain time and at a certain place. Such morality is different from ethics, and thus is called social morality. On the other hand, ethics has two meanings: the first of which refers to the principles that are directly or indirectly drawn from the knowledge of human's value. In its second meaning, ethics is a discipline of philosophy which presents or at least expected to present verifiable information in ethical issues concerning humans.[32]

The role of equity in filling the gaps in a statute and exercising the power of discretion is of particular importance. I concluded from the judges' responses that equity is most often understood or perceived as "satisfied conviction". A considerably large portion of the judges mentioned "eased conscience" and "satisfaction of the parties in a case". This is a conceptualization which points to the period before the stage in the evolution of the concept of conscientious conviction, when logic and reason were adopted as guides.[33] Some of the judges stated that they made equitable decisions once they achieved impartiality. Yet, the interviewees most often mentioned equity with reference to the conditions of a particular case. Among these, only a few perceived the conditions of a particular case as the personal situation of the parties and

---

[30] loc. Cit.
[31] Hans-Georg Gadamer, "The Problem of Historical Consciousness", in *Interpretive Social Science: A Reader*, Paul Rabinow, William Sullivan ed., 1979, p. 156.
[32] Uygur, *Law, Ethics and Principles*, p. 2.
[33] Metin Feyzioğlu, *Conscience (Personal Convict) in Penal Jurisdiction*, 2002, pp. 21—38.

their particular contexts. Another surprising observation was the considerably high rate of those who perceived and expressed these conditions as customary law, a significant part of whom were criminal judges. Of my interviewees, a considerable number of criminal judges stated that they considered in their decisions the conditions of a particular case, which also contained the rules of customary law; therefore they considered these rules when implementing the law, although they are not accepted as one of the sources in criminal procedure. At this juncture, it won't be wrong to say that a lot of interviewees' equity perceptions are shaped by pre-understandings which prevail against the conditions of particular case, ethic, the certain meaning of the written law and justice. In some examples which were told by the interviewees about the judicial decision making process, these pre-understandings become as final decision directly. They tell these cases as good experiences of equity judgment.[34]

Since Holmes said "the life of the law has not been logic: it has been experience. (...) what the courts declare to have always been the law is in fact new."[35] Phrase "how judges think" is one of the most interesting questions of empirical legal studies. Although the claim of legal realists that gives the legislative role to the courts seems problematic with the democratic principals and legal certainty[36], it evokes the interest to the structural analysis of the judicial process. Describing the role of equity and the equity perceptions of judges in enactment as "a value jurisprudence does not exalt judges to a role that they do not have now, but rather recognizes their existing role for what it is".[37]

As mentioned above, the subject of this paper is limited to the presentation of a preliminary analysis and the first codes on the data obtained from the field. There-

---

[34] For an empirical legal study analyzing the pre-understandings as a resource of subjectivity in judicial process see Mithat Sancar, Eylem Ümit Atılgan, "*Justice can be Bypassed Sometimes*" : *Judges and Prosecutors in the Democratization Process*, 2009.

[35] Oliver Wendell Holmes, "The Common Law", in *The Mind and Faith of Justice Holmes, His Speeches, Essays, Letters and Judicial Opinions*, Max Lerner ed., 1989, p. 51, p. 54.

[36] For an evaluation of legal realism and different approaches separate from the main stream see Ülker Gürkan, "Legal Realism", *Ankara University Law Faculty Periodicals* 225, 1967.

[37] For the concept of value jurisprudence see Joshua B. Shiffrin, "A Practical Jurisprudence of Values: Re-Writing Lechmere, Inc. v. NLRB", in *Harvard Civil Rights-Civil Liberties Law Review*, V. 41, 2006, p. 186.

fore, it serves as an introduction to a comprehensive study. In the subsequent stages of the study, considerably rich data obtained from in-depth interviews will possibly give way to a multidimensional analysis in various interpretational contexts and in the light of detailed codes.

Doctrinal Knowledge and Interdisciplinary Studies of Law: A Reflection on Methodology

Chia-yin Chang

I. Preamble

The interdisciplinary approach to the study of law (interdisciplinary legal studies) has become the focal point in academic law recently. Taiwanese academic programs[1] use "科际整合" (pronounced as "ke-ji-zheng-he") to describe this trend, and in China it is called "交叉学科研究" (pronounced as jiao-cha-xue-ke-yan-jiu). A more accurate Chinese translation should be "跨学科研究" (kua-xue-ke-yan-jiu) or "科际合作" (ke-ji-he-zuo). This new legal study approach is a reflective and critical perspective on traditional legal studies and methodology. Therefore, this trend implies some defects in traditional legal studies. Is that true? To what extent can we say that there must be some defects existing in tranditional legal

---

[1] In fact, many universities in Taiwan also establish the graduate institute with similar name such as the Graduate Institute of Interdisciplinary Legal Studies in Taiwan University and the Institute of Law and Inter-discipline in Chengchi University.

study? What is the standard we use when making this judgment? Those are questions we can keep on investigating.

Of course, it's true that co-operating other disciplines will expand the vision of academic legal community, and it might even lead to a fundamental critique on the assumptions about law. Here are the main issues: What kind of the influence do those interdisciplinary approachs and achievements have on jurisprudence? Are those achievements able to be internalized and digested by jurisprudence? How can jurisprudence make use of this new knowledge? In other words, what is the essence of the interdisciplinary approach to law? Is there any specific method existing in the interdisciplinary approach for jurisprudence that should be adopted?

II. Jurisprudence as Legal Dogmatics

1. The Concept of Jurisprudence

The concept of jurisprudence has some corresponding terms such as *Jurisprudenz* and *Rechtswissenschaft* (legal science) in German. Although *Jurisprudenz* and *Rechtswissenschaft* are regarded as synonymous terms [2], the term *Jurisprudenz* has another meaning. The term *Jurisprudenz* sometimes refers to the concept of *Rechtsphilosophie* (legal philosophy). Therefore *Jurisprudenz* has wider meaning than *Rechtswissenschaft*.

Rechtsdogmatik (legal dogmatics) is often regarded as a core concept in *Rechtswissenschaft*.[3] Gustav Radbruch, a famous German legal scholar, said the essence of *Rechtswissenschaft* is the "*systematische, dogmatische Rechtswissenschaft*"[4] (the systematic and dogmatic legal science), and Ralf Dreier describes legal dog-

---

[2] See Eric Hilgendorf, "Zur Lage der juristischen Grundlagenforschung in Deutschland heute", in *Rechtsphilosophie im 21. Jahrhundert*, Winfried Brugger, Ulrich Neumann and Stephan Kirste ed., Suhrkamp, 2008, p.111 and Note 1; see also Ralf Dreier, "Zum Selbstverständnis der Jurisprudenz als Wissenschaft", in *Recht—Moral—Ideologie. Studien zur Rechtstheorie*, Suhrkamp, 1981, p.5. Thomas Vesting cites many juristic works during the nineteenth and the twentieth century to argue that the thought of dividing legal dogmatics and jurisprudence did not appear until last two centuries. See Thomas Vesting, *Rechtstheorie: Ein Studienbuch*, Beck Juristischer Verlag, 2007, p.10.

[3] See Oliver Lepsius, "Themen einer Rechtswissenschaftstheorie", in *Rechtswissenschaftstheorie*, Mtthias Jestaedt and Oliver Lepsius ed., Mohr Siebeck, 2008, pp.16—17.

[4] Gustav Radbruch, *Rechtsphilosophie*, C.F. Müller, 1999, p.106.

matics as "die Kerndisziplin der Rechtswissenschaft[5]" (the kernel of legal science). The fact that legal domagtics could be the core of legal science shows that legal science also contains other intellectual activities besides of legal dogmatics. This inference can be proved by various courses in law school. Generally speaking, the curriculum in law school contains two parts. One part is the curriculum about the substantial and procedural law on civil, criminal, and public law. The other part includes courses such as philosophy of law, sociology of law, law and psychology, law and economics, law and history, and methodology of law. We can call the former part the dogmatic discipline[6], dogmatic jurisprudence, or the legal science on the application of law[7] and the other part the basic research of law[8]. Therefore besides referring to legal dogmatics, the concept of *Rechtswissenschaft* also incorporates basic research of law. The concept of *Rechtswissenschaft* is then regarded as a term that includes several dogmatic disciplines and basic research of law.[9]

---

[5] Ralf Dreier, "Zum Selbstverständnis der Jurisprudenz als Wissenschaft", in *Recht—Moral—Ideologie. Studien zur Rechtstheorie*, Suhrkamp, 1981, p. 51; Ralf Dreier, "Rechtstheorie und Rechtsgeschichte", in *Recht-Staat-Vernunft: Studien zur Rechtstheorie 2*, Suhrkamp, 1991, p. 217. When we claim the core of jurisprudence is the legal dogmatics, the distinction of the core and the periphery is implied in it. Maybe someone will question whether this distinction decreases the values of the other approaches in law. This question presupposes that the distinction between the core and the periphery is equal to the distinction between the higher and the lower value, the mainstream and the non-mainstream, and the orthodox and the heterodox. When we claim the "core meaning" of jurisprudence is legal dogmatics, what we want to do is to clarify the property of knowledge and the logic of jurisprudence, and not to evaluate what kind of knowledge on constitutional law has higher value. It needs further investigation to see if this claim will influence the power logic in academic field and cause the disciplines posited in the frontier to be harmed by the "orthodox". Of course, knowledge is also power, but the operation of academic power is limited by many conditions in reality and the claim of "the core of jurisprudence is the legal dogmatics" is one of the conditions at least. The key point of this claim is doubtful.

[6] See Oliver Lepsius, "Themen einer Rechtswissenschaftstheorie", in *Rechtswissenschaftstheorie*, p. 9.

[7] See Anne van Aaken, "Funktionale Rechtswissenschaftstheorie für die gesamte Rechtswissenschaft", in *Rechtswissenschaftstheorie*, p. 79.

[8] See Eric Hilgendorf, "Zur Lage der juristischen Grundlagenforschung in Deutschland heute", in *Rechtsphilosophie im 21. Jahrhundert*, Winfried Brugger, Ulrich Neumann and Stephan Kirste ed., Suhrkamp, 2008, p. 111.

[9] Professor Yen, Chueh-An discusses the character of legal science from the concept of the positive science and uses the distinction of internal and external point to distinguish between "jurisprudence A" and "jurisprudence B". The former indicates that the jurisprudence from the participant's view treating norm with binding force and the latter indicates the jurisprudence from the observer's view to describe and explain the legal norm, legal system, and the general character of law. He calls the two types the "positive legal science" and argues the alternative jurisprudence. See Yen, Chueh-An, "The Construction of Norm and the Argumentation", in *Norm, Argument, and Action-The Collected Works on Epistemology of Law*, Angle, 2004, pp. 20—31.

There are some questions worth further investigating. First of all, there is the question about the core meaning of *Rechtswissenschaft*. Although the kernel of *Rechtswissenschaft* is legal dogmatics, the meaning of legal dogmatics (the character, function, and limitation of legal dogmatics) needs to be explained further. Even though empirically and conceptually legal dogmatics is the core of legal science, is it worth maintaining this argument? In other words, will it narrow the scope of legal science or harm the development of jurisprudence if we redefine legal science as legal dogmatics? Furthermore, is legal dogmatics itself the subject entitled to be criticized? Secondly, it is the question about the relationship between these different kinds of knowledge within legal science. For example, what are the relationships between legal dogmatics and the basic research of law? Is it a kind of functional division within legal science? Or does it not only separate the two but also exclude the other? Does the functional differentiation mean to perform each function without any co-operation? Or does it mean that there may be some possibilities of collaborating, which we call the possibility of the interdisciplinary collaboration? What is much more interesting is that if the two belong to the concept of legal science at the same time and are accepted by legal professors in the institutional framework, how can it result in the co-exclusion relationship? Why, and can it be improved?

It will also feed back to the reformation of legal education[10], which is still growing now, if we reflect on the matter about legal dogmatics, the basic research of law, and the relationship between them. The question of what is legal science is relevant to the question of what kind of lawyers we do expect because law school is just the institutional medium between legal science and the legal profession.[11]

---

[10] This trend in Asia has caused lots of disputes about whether to establish the postgraduate law school or not. In fact, Japan has legislated the relevant enactment in 2004 and South Korea also follows. Due to the resistance from many law schools, Taiwan didn't pass the draft.

[11] Here is implying another question: which function does jurisprudence perform. More exactly what kind of function does legal dogmatics, legal theory, and the scientific observation on law perform?

2. The Character of Jurisprudence

There are different characterizations of jurisprudence.[12] The most familiar and well-known characterization is that of humanities (*Geisteswissenschaft*)[13] and some characterize it as factual science (*Realwissenschaft*).

It is the tradition for German jurisprudence to define itself as a part of the humanities since 20th century.[14] Radbruch defines jurisprudence as "the understandable science of culture" (*vestehende Kulturwissenschaft*) with three main characters: the understandable, the individualized, and the value-related (*wertbeziehend*) characters.[15] He argues that basically jurisprudence is a systematic and dogmatic legal science, which is the science of investigating the objective meaning of positive legal order.[16] He thinks the object of jurisprudence is the positive law and jurisprudence is the science about the valid law, not about the right law (das richtige Recht). It's the science about what *law is*, not about what law *ought to be*. Jurisprudence deals with the legal order and legal norms, not the legal fact or the legal life. Jurisprudence is the science about the objective meaning of law, not the subjective meaning. Therefore, jurisprudence, whose characters are dogmatic and systematic, proceeds in three steps: interpretation, construction, and systematization.[17] Given Radbruch's arguments, there remain two questions to be answered. First, what is the *being of law*? In other words, what is the validity of the valid law? Second, how can it be possible for the epistemology of law if jurisprudence is the science of being relevant to value instead of not value-blinded and evaluative?

The characterization of jurisprudence by Karl Larenz, a German legal scholar on civil law, may be the representative of the approach to humanities. In fact, Larenz

---

[12] Compare to Ralf Dreier, "Zum Selbstverständnis der Jurisprudenz als Wissenschaft", in *Recht—Moral—Ideologie. Studien zur Rechtstheorie*, Suhrkamp, 1981, pp. 51—56; Dreier distinguishes two opinions: the conception of legal positivism and the conception of sociology. Dreier himself builds the conception with three dimensions and claims the plural functions of jurisprudence.

[13] Translated as "science of spirit" also.

[14] Compare to Ralf Dreier, "Zum Selbstverständnis der Jurisprudenz als Wissenschaft", in *Recht—Moral—Ideologie. Studien zur Rechtstheorie*, p. 50.

[15] Gustav Radbruch, *Rechtsphilosophie*, C. F. Müller, 1999, p. 115.

[16] Ibid., p. 106.

[17] Ibid., pp. 106—115.

never uses the concept of humanities. Instead, he calls legal science as "the science of the norm". He also regards jurisprudence and legal dogmatics as synonymous terms.[18] The reason for calling legal science as the science of the norm is that jurisprudence focuses on the positive legal norms and the content of legal judgments in the normative dimension. For him, jurisprudence is a kind of system of statements about valid laws. Jurisprudence pays attention to the normative validity, that is, the binding force, not the factual validity, not the efficacy, and not the probability of application which sociology of law focuses on.[19] Statements in jurisprudence are different from statements in natural sciences. These statements are different from the kind of statements about facts dependent on sensation or on observable facts, although it is necessary for jurisprudence to rely on the sensational process when it makes the statements about the legal validity and the content of legal norms.[20] Another German legal scholar, Karl Engisch, also maintains that the statements about things sensational are either "true" or "false" and the statements about the validity are either "right" or "wrong"[21].

This article places Karl Larenz's approach in the context of humanities. The reason is that he regards jurisprudence as the "understandable" science ("*verstehende Wissenschaft*"), which is in the traditional context of humanities and hermeneutics since Schleiermacher. For Larenz, the main field which jurisprudence focuses on is linguistic expressions such as the normative meaning of legal texts including legal statues, legal judgments, administrative actions, and contracts. Through reflective mediating action, "interpretation" ("*Auslegen*"), jurisprudence can obtain the meaning of texts. For the meaning of texts, the "interpretation" could obtain more than one consequence by logical reasoning. The interpretation is a kind of choice between different possible meanings based on reasoning[22]. For Larenz, the reason

---

[18] Karl Larenz, *Methodenlehre der Rechtswissenschaft*, Springer, 1991, pp. 189—193.
[19] Ibid., p. 195.
[20] Ibid., p. 196.
[21] Karl Engisch, "Wahrheit und Richtigkeit im juristischen Denken", in *Beitäge zur Rechtstheorie*, Klostermann, 1984, p. 287. (cited from n. 18, above, p. 198). It is an important issue of discussing whether there is true/falsef value or not in legal statements for the comtemporary legal philosophy. The purpose of this article citing the opinion of Karl Engisch, the famous German legal scholar, is to indicate this opinion has been the mainstream in the German legal academic.
[22] See Karl Larenz, *Methodenlehre der Rechtswissenschaft*, p. 204.

why jurisprudence is a kind of science is that in principle jurisprudence can problematize legal texts, or in other words it can reflectively investigate different interpretations.[23]

Hans Albert[24], a critical rationalist, uses the concept of the factual science to describe jurisprudence. He knows the traditional distinction between the sciences very well. What jurisprudence faces is the norm, not *being of law*, and what jurisprudence seeks is the understanding, not the explanation. Therefore, the activities of jurisprudence are totally different from the so-called scientific activities and adopt different methods.[25] The revelant legal norms in a case are the "dogma" for lawyers. They are given and necessary to be accepted by lawyers. What lawyers do is to find the meaning of the leagl norms. This is also the mission of hermeneutics as the science of correct interpretation. Jurisprudence is opposite of factual sciences in this meaning. It is a dogmatic, normative, and hermeneutic discipline.[26] Albert, however, thinks that it is possible for jurisprudence to be a the factual science. If, according to Albert, law is a kind of social reality, the constitutive part of social life, then this kind of science will be the social science.[27]

Albert seems to think even if jurisprudence involves the valid norms it does not necessarily result in a dogmatic character. Even if jurisprudence deals with the valid norms in fact, it is not necessary to regard norms as the binding standards and not necessary to be related to a normative claim. Furthermore, to discuss and to investigate norms does not presuppose the normative science, and it can be like the factual science regarding norms as the constitutive conditions of social regulation and steering instead. Making use of the method of understanding character does not necessarily lead to a special charaterization of science.[28]

Albert seems to think there is nothing different even if someone agrees that juris-

---

[23] Ibid., p. 204.
[24] In the past so-called "sociological jurisprudence" (*soziologische Jurisprudenz*) or the legal realism (*der juristische Realismus*) also located jurisprudence in the context of the natural sciences. See Ralf Dreier, "Zum Selbstverständnis der Jurisprudenz als Wissenschaft", in *Recht—Moral—Ideologie. Studien zur Rechtstheorie*, p. 50.
[25] Hans Albert, *Rechtswissenschaft als Realwissenschaft*, Nomos, 1993, p. 8.
[26] Ibid., p. 9.
[27] Ibid., p. 7.
[28] Ibid., pp. 10—11.

prudence, which is different from sociology of law, is a kind of science oriented toward praxis whose mission is not the explanation, but the preparation for adjudication. Because jurisprudence is like a techology, a system of statements about the possibilities of actions dependent on theoretical statements of effects-interdependency. Those statements do not indicate agents what should be done, but what can be done to reach some certain purpose. Therefore Albert suggests we can regard jurisprudence as social techology whose purpose is the preparation of specific social decisions.[29] There is another epistemological reason for Albert's argument. Hans Albert doesn't think the so-called normative cognition exists. Even if it does exist, the normative cognition has an epistemological character and is of true/false value. That means it is not real normative cognition. What the legal reasoning indicates is just the logical question of judging the correct reasoning in the normative statements, and not the real normative question of epistemology.[30] As a result, the mission of jurisprudence is to know the valid law in fact by dogmatic methods and to set up the foundation for appropriate decisions, or in other words, the appropriate operations of relevant norms.[31] Albert advocates a new concept of factual validity which is not defined as the efficacy or the probability of application but as the relevance to the will of the norm-maker. The will is going to influence the norm addressee to have a reason fulfilling the actions which the norm-maker requires. Because it is the causal meaning, the factual validity belongs to the social reality and the statements involved with the validity are of cognitive character.[32]

Jurisprudence, of course, is a kind of science focusing on legal norms and we can call it the science of the norm. However, it is a question of whether jurisprudence is a normative science or a factual science. This question involves three basic questions. The first one is the possibility of normative cognition. Secondly, it connects to a special question: Is it possible to cancel the distinction between the normative validity and the factual validity or even to cancel the concept of normative validity due to the new concept of factual validity advocated by Albert? Thirdly, is it pos-

---

[29] Ibid., p. 12.
[30] Ibid., pp. 13—14.
[31] Ibid., p. 15.
[32] Ibid., p. 20.

sible to have statements in jurisprudence without connecting the normative requirement? It seems that the evaluation (*Wertung*) is a necessary part of traditional jurisprudence.[33] Albert, however, insists that the evaluation can be regarded as the cognition[34], but is it necessary to become involved with evaluation in the interpretation and application of law, or can we establish the rational jurisprudence[35] by excluding evaluation from the field of jurisprudence?

3. Legal Dogmatics

This article will observe the characters of legal dogmatic in three dimensions: the un-dominated object, the applied-orientation, and conceptuality and the systematization.

Legal dogmatics is "the science of investigating the objective meaning on positive legal order" (Radbruch) and is a kind of "system of statements about the valid law" (Larenz). The object of legal dogmatics is the valid positive legal norm, and the positive legal norm is also the dogma, which is in the key point for legal dogmatics. The reason why legal dogmatics is called legal dogmatics is that this discipline presupposes un-dominated objects.[36] Even without any connection with the dogmatism, legal dogmatics still is able to criticize legal norms. However, in principle the criticism is within the legal system and legal dogmatics does not question the whole valid legal system where it belongs.[37]

Besides that, legal dogmatics has two other meanings. We can know an important character of legal dogmatics from another similar concept, that is, the science of

---

[33] Karl Larenz, *Methodenlehre der Rechtswissenschaft*, pp. 214—229; Robert Alexy takes the inevitability of the evaluation as his starting point of the theory of legal argumentation. See Robert Alexy, *Theorie der juristischen Argumentation. Die Theorie des rationalen Diskurses als Theorie der juristischen Begründung*, Suhrkamp, 1991, pp. 24—31.

[34] Hans Albert, *Rechtswissenschaft als Realwissenschaft*, p. 36.

[35] The term which Hans Albert uses, see Ibid., p. 24.

[36] Werner Heun, "Begriff, Eigenart, Methoden der Verfassungsrechtsdogmatik", in *Die Rolle der Verfassungsrechtswissenschaft im demokratischen Verfassungsstaat*, Christian Starck ed., Nomos, 2004, p. 38; Karl-E. Hain, "Systematische Rekonstruktion des Verfassungsrechts als Aufgabe der Verfassungsrechtsdogmatik", in *Die Rolle der Verfassungsrechtswissenschaft im demokratischen Verfassungsstaat*, p. 47.

[37] Arthur Kaufmann, "Rechtsphilosophie, Rechtstheorie, Rechtsdogmatik", in *Einführung in Rechtsphilosophie und Rechtstheorie der Gegenwart*, Arthur Kaufmann and Winfried Hassemer ed., UTB Uni-Taschenbücher, 2004, p. 2.

law-applied (*Rechtsanwendungswissenschaft*). The important character is that legal dogmatics is oriented toward resolving questions in every case, and to deal with the form of the formulation in legal rules and the concept of law to reach the preciseness and exactness. In other words, the purpose of legal dogmatics is to determine the norm involved in a case and the meaning of concepts so that it can be applied in other cases without difficulty.[38] This meaning of legal dogmatics expresses the necessity of the conceptual argumentation in the world of law.[39]

In the context of German legal thinking, legal dogmatics has another more ambitious meaning. After the German historical jurisprudence developed, legal dogmatics became connected with the concept of system. In the early period, it was even connected with the mechanical picture of the world. According to this view of point, it demanded that all the legal materials could be delimited hierarchically, systematized logically, and finally ended in one first principle.[40] This kind of systematization has already been discarded. For example, Radbruch thinks jurisprudence deals with materials of law from the concept and teleology. The former regards law as the realization of the concept of law and the latter as the realization of the idea of law. The dual process is called the construction (*Konstruktion*) when jurisprudence deals with the specific and particular legal system. The dual process is called the system (*System*) when it is relevant to the whole legal order.[41] It is not the first question of how to define the concept of system.[42] This kind of meaning of legal dogmatics indicates the necessity of systematic argumentation.[43]

Some scholars, such as Robert Alexy, define the character of legal dogmatic in three dimensions. The first dimension is the analytic which involves with the analysis of conceptuality and systematization about the valid law, such as the analysis of basic concepts, the construction of law, and the structure of legal system.[44] The second is the empirical dimension which involves with the epistemology of valid legal norms

---

[38] Thomas Vesting, *Rechtstheorie:Ein Studienbuch*, Beck Juristischer, 2007, pp. 11—12.
[39] Niklas Luhmann, *Das Recht der Gesellschaft*, Suhrkamp, 1993, p. 387 (cited from Ibid., p. 12).
[40] Thomas Vesting, *Rechtstheorie:Ein Studienbuch*, p. 12.
[41] Gustav Radbruch, *Rechtsphilosophie*, p. 113.
[42] See Karl Larenz, *Methodenlehre der Rechtswissenschaft*, pp. 437—441; See p. 473 about the discussion of the external/abstract system of concept and the internal system.
[43] Thomas Vesting, *Rechtstheorie:Ein Studienbuch*, p. 12.
[44] Robert Alexy, *Theorie der Grundrechte*, p. 23.

focusing on the description of statutes and adjudications. It also involves with the efficacy of law because the efficiency is the precondition for the positive validity of statutes and adjudications.[45] The empirical dimension, however, does not include all the observable facts. It involves facts whose connection is indicated by law.[46] The third is the normative dimension which is not only digging out the positive legal norms, but also paying attention to guide and criticize the court's decisions. What it cares about is the correct decision based on positive legal rule in a case so that it will involve with the evaluation. In this dimension, legal dogmatics focuses on how to make rational and justifiable decisions about the evaluation.[47] During the history of jurisprudence, the three dimensions have their own weight. However, Alexy thinks that jurisprudence as a practical discipline is oriented towards the resolution of what ought to be done in a case. Therefore, it must be a discipline integrated into the three dimensions, and the combination of those dimensions is the necessary condition for the rationality in jurisprudence.[48] The analytic dimension Alexy discusses is similar to the argumentation of the concept and of the system. The empirical one has the un-dominated character because legal dogmatics takes the positive and valid legal norms as its starting point (the so-called "dogma"). The normative dimension and the practical discipline partly respond to the case-oriented character.

Since legal dogmatics takes the positive and valid legal norms as its starting point and treats the text as "dogma", it presupposes the binding force and authority of the legal text. Therefore, the mission of legal dogmatics is to interpret legal norms and to discuss the rationality or correctness when legal norms apply to a concrete case. In the end, legal dogmatics still needs to face the question of validity. What is the validity of legal norms? [49] This question involves at least three inter-connected dimensions. Valid legal norms must be recognized at the empirical dimension. No matter if it is the legal rule or the legal principle incorporated into the statutes and

---

[45] Ibid., p. 23.
[46] Compare to ibid., pp. 24—25.
[47] Ibid., p. 25.
[48] Ibid., pp. 26—27.
[49] About the discussion on the relationship between the validity of law and the epistemology of law see Yen, Chueh-An, "The Validity of Law and the Interpretation of Law-Reflection on the Character of Jurisprudence from Habermas's and Kaufmann's theory of legal validity", in *Collected Works on Legal Philosophy and Political Thoughts*, Angle, 2005, pp. 131—152.

the precedents, they must be presented by the object caught through sensation. Legal dogmatics must be capable of describing the empirically valid legal norm.[50] However, not all the objects presented in this way will be recognized as legal norms, the legal norms which are accepted and identified by certain communities (especially the legal community). Then the analytic and normative dimensions take effect jointly in this process [51], and the real legal norm can be picked out from the empirically recognized legal norms prima facie. Then the content of the meaning will be confirmed through the interpretation. At this stage, the process is going to be closely relevant to legal philosophy, as Dworkin claims in *Law's Empire*:

> So no firm line divides jurisprudence from adjudication or any other aspect of legal practice. Legal philosophers debate about the general part, the interpretive foundation any legal argument must have. We may turn that coin over. Any practical legal argument, no matter how detailed and limited, assumes the kind of abstract foundation jurisprudence offers, and when rival foundations compete, a legal argument assumes one and rejects others. So any judge's opinion is itself a piece of legal philosophy, even when the philosophy is hidden and the visible argument is dominated by citation and lists of facts. Jurisprudence is the general part of adjudication, silent prologue to any decision at law.[52]

Indeed, the legal practice always presupposes the understanding and the paradigm of law offered by legal philosophy, and legal dogmatics can't avoid of this general part. This connection is always hidden during the process of interpreting and applying the norm. The general part will not be discussed until we face hard cases. This is because the external justification in legal argumentation often proceeds by way of the operation of conceptuality and legal dogmatics is the basic threshold to prevent thematizing the fundamental questions. This is also an important function of legal dogmatics: to keep the court away from the fundamental questions, that is, the questions of evaluation and the substantial questions about principles.

---

[50] Ralf Dreier, "Zum Selbstverständnis der Jurisprudenz als Wissenschaft", in *Recht—Moral—Ideologie. Studien zur Rechtstheorie*, p. 53.

[51] The question of validity will be hidden until it is thematized. Because the norm is recognized as a legal norm by its legal community at the same time the validity is also confirmed and only in the next moment the question of validity can be offered through the process of reflection.

[52] Ronald Dworkin, *Law's Empire*, Belknep Press of Harvard University Press, 1986, p. 90.

We still face the question unsolved after describing the characters of legal dogmatic, that is, jurisprudence (legal dogmatics) is a kind of science. And what is a science? Similar to Larenz's claim, Alexy regards jurisprudence (legal dogmatics) as a practical discipline and in the end it needs to resolve the question of what it ought to be. Even if we suspend the dispute about science temporarily, legal dogmatics still has to face the problem of its rationality. On one side, if legal dogmatics can't escape from evaluation, then how does legal dogmatics develop its rationality or correctness of the argumentation? This question leads to the study of methodology of law and the theory of the legal argumentation investigating the correctly interpreting procedure, and to forms and rules of argumentation. On the other side, if legal dogmatics takes the valid legal norm as its main object, then legal dogmatics has to deal with the question of interpretation of facts in life because of the valid legal norms contains many concepts connoting facts. However, legal dogmatics can't reach the goal simply by using the method of interpretation. Regarding this point, how can legal dogmatics develop its rationality or correctness of argumentation? This leads to the critique of jurisprudence and the requirement of the so-called interdisciplinary study of law.

The discussion above is based on the concept of legal dogmatics in the context of German legal thinking. It may be challenged by questioning the universality of its claim. The tension of this challenge can be loosened by further explanation. Although at first glance, German legal dogmatics indeed emphasizes systematization and even takes the system of legal dogmatics as its ultimate purpose and this makes it unique. Radbruch mentions the three steps for developing jurisprudence, and the final step is the system when he talks about the logic of law. But maybe the unique part is a matter of degree. What is important is not that whether it can develop the system or not. What is important is whether or not it is necessary to have systematic argumentation. Obviously, it is inevitable to question the consistence and coherence for any kind of jurisprudence pursuing the rationality so that the systematic argumentation is unavoidable. The universality of legal dogmatics is not built upon any abstract theory but upon the similarity of legal reasoning in different legal cultures. Legal reasoning takes the valid legal norm as its starting point, investigates the meaning of legal norms, and applies norms to the concrete cases. Jurisprudence based on the logic and structure of legal reasoning also shares the characteristics of legal dogmatics mentioned above.

III. The Interdisciplinary Study of Law

There is still a question about whether the object of research is the same once jurisprudence takes a different method rather than that of the legal dogmatics. The object of research is constructed differently by different method. So something like the object of research doesn't exist before it is recognized or constructed. Traditional jurisprudence takes the investigation of the normative meaning as its main focus. It achieves its goal through the interpretation of texts. The other science, especially those belonging to the social sciences, however, emphasizes positive or empirical characteristics of the social phenomena, so even if it is interesting to investigate the phenomena of law. What it focuses on is not the normative meaning of the text but the reality of law. It seems that there are two possibilities for the interdisciplinary study of law. The first one is to integrate other disciplines into jurisprudence. The second is to integrate jurisprudence into other disciplines. For the interdisciplinary study of law, starting from jurisprudence, only the former is possible. The latter means studies of other disciplines on law.

The thesis that the core of jurisprudence is legal dogmatic is difficult to challenge, even if legal dogmatics is not self-sufficient and needs to be supported by legal philosophy and the social sciences, especially in terms of values and facts. The question is still the same, even if the USA doesn't have a strong tradition of legal dogmatics like Germany. The question is how the perspective of the other disciplines to be integrated into jurisprudence. The main point is not how to replace the construction of jurisprudence by the other disciplines. For the meaning of statutes and adjudications is still the studying subject for jurisprudence, no matter how it can be analyzed from different theoretical perspectives.[53]

---

[53] From 1965 to 1985, the German academics had developed a trend of studying on legal theories with different kinds of approaches. It was different from the traditional legal philosophy of right law (*richtiges Recht*) and just law (*gerechtes Recht*). It focused on the analysis of various legal concepts on one side and the construction of the inter-disciplines (*interdisziplinäre*) on the other side. It attempted to bridge the gap between social science, psychology, and natural science and jurisprudence. See Eric Hilgendorf, "Zur Lage der juristischen Grundlagenforschung in Deutschland heute", in *Rechtsphilosophie im 21. Jahrhundert*, Winfried Brugger, Ulrich Neumann and Stephan Kirste ed., Suhrkamp, 2008, pp. 112—113.

Since the legal dogmatics has been built on various forms of legal argumentation, we can use the theory of the legal argumentation to discuss the construction of knowledge in jurisprudence. Generally speaking, the mission of legal argumentation is to investigate the legal justification and the justification of premises it uses. It emphasizes the function of subsumption to the justification of decisions in law and divides the structure of justification into two parts: internal and external justification.[54] The former indicates the structure of the logical inference. The latter indicates the justification of the premise used in the process of deduction. The forms of legal argumentations can be distinguished, as Robert Alexy has suggested: the linguistic argument, the genetic argument, the systematic argument, and the general practical argument.[55] The first three is also called as the institutional argument because they are founded in the institutional framework of legal system, whose authority is rooted in positive law. In contrast to the institutional argument, the general practical argument and the substantial argument focus on the correctness of the content.[56] In a case when no decision can be made, or in the same case when more than one decision is supported by institutional arguments, it will be dependent on the substantial evaluations to make the final decision. When the institutional arguments cannot

---

[54] This is a common framework for justification, but there may be different framework being used. Alexy calls it as the internal and external justification (See Robert Alexy, *Theorie der juristischen Argumentation. Die Theorie des rationalen Diskurses als Theorie der juristischen Begründung*, p. 273) and other scholars call it the justification of the first and second order or the main scheme (*Hauptschemata*) and the subordinate scheme (*Nebenschemata*). See Hans-Joachim Koch/Helmut Rüßmann, *Juristische Begründungslehre. Eine Einführung in Grundprobleme der Rechtswissenschaft*, C. H. Beck, 1986, p. 6; Ulrich Neumann, *Juristische Argumentation* Wiesenschaftliche Buchgesellschaft, 1986, p. 80; Aulis Aarnio, *The Rational as Reasonable:A Treatise on Legal Justification*, Springer, 1987, p. 119.

[55] Here is the brief: the linguistic argument includes the semantic (*semantisch*) and syntactic (*syntaktisch*) arguments; the genetic argument includes the subjective-semantic (*subjektiv-semantisch*) and subjective-teleological (*subjektiv-teleologisch*) arguments; the systematic argument is divided into eight kinds including the consistent (*konsistenzsichernd*), contextual (*kontextuell*); conceptual-systematic (*begrifflich-systematisch*), special (*speziell juristisch*), precedential (*präjudiziell*), historical (*historisch*), comparative argument (*komparativ*), and the argument of the principle (*Prinzipienargument*); the general practical argument is divided into two parts: the teleological argument (*teleologische Argumente*) oriented to the consequence of interpretation and the deontological argument (*deontologische Argumente*) founded in the concept of oughtness. See Robert Alexy, "Juristische Interpretation", in *Recht, Vernunft, Diskurs*, Suhrkamp, 1995, pp. 84—85; Robert Alexy, *Theorie der juristischen Argumentation. Die Theorie des rationalen Diskurses als Theorie der juristischen Begründung*, p. 285.

[56] See Robert Alexy, "Juristische Interpretation", in *Recht, Vernunft, Diskurs*, p. 88.

lead to a rational external justification, no matter what facts or the level of normativity, it is necessary to use the general practical argument.[57] The general practical argument has always appeared as the substantial reasoning of the evaluation. Sometimes a conflict of evaluations does not result from the choice between values; it comes from the different judgments on the facts. This is the reason why legal dogmatics needs to be supported by other disciplines. In this context, the interdisciplinary study of law can be regarded as the attempt to find the appropriate position of the other disciplines in legal dogmatics or to find out their possible contribution to legal dogmatics.

In the construction of doctinal knowledge in leagl dogmatics, it will deal with not only the normative arguments but also the cognitive arguments in the teleological argument (the general practical argument). This is obvious for the consequential argument.[58] The precondition of the consequential argument is the description and the prediction of the consequence according to the social sciences, although there can not be absolute certainty for any prediction. The prediction with the hypothetical character is still a true/false value. In other words, we still can decide the truth and falseness of a prediction even without absolute certainty.[59] The cognitive dimension of the consequential argument is called the empirical argument because it works at an empirical level. Therefore, the issue is to introduce the empirical knowledge or the knowledge of empirical science during the construction of legal dogmatics. Therefore, jurisprudence is open to the study of the empirical science in some extent and we can find the demand for bridging the normative and factual argumentation.

However, the process of constructing legal knowledge is hermeneutical. The hermeneutic circle is inherent in all of the hermeneutical activities. Even the empiri-

---

[57] Ibid, p. 87.

[58] Discussion on the consequential argument see Gunther Teubner, "Folgenorientierung", in *Entscheidungsfolgen als Rechtsgründe*, Gunther Teubner ed. , Nomos, 1995, pp. 9—16; Niklas Luhmann, "Juristische Argumentation: eine Analyse ihrer Form" , in *Entscheidungsfolgen als Rechtsgründe*, pp. 19—37; Dieter Grimm, "Entscheidungsfolgen als Rechtsgründe: Zur Argumentationspraxis des deutschen Bundesverfassungsgerichts" , in *Entscheidungsfolgen als Rechtsgründe*, pp. 139—159; Martina R. Deckert, *Folgenorientierung in der Rechtsanwendung*, C. H. Beck, 1995.

[59] See Hans Albert, *Rechtswissenschaft als Realwissenschaft: Das Recht als soziale Tatsache und die Aufgabe der Jurisprudenz*, p. 30.

cal argument is not simply the purely empirical proposition, but also a statement about facts containing abundant theoretical perspectives. Therefore, the reflection on the legal dogmatics can be traced to an important level: The background presuppositions of the legal reasoning. Such reflections also include the social picture presupposed by the legal interpretation and argumentation.

Finally, there is another possible relationship between legal dogmatics and the other disciplines. The point is not the "integration" of different types of knowledge. The point is how legal dogmatics co-operates with the other disciplines. The "co-operation" may be constructive or critical, and it may even be deconstructive. In fact, the insight offered by empirical sciences often subverts common sense. Because the interpretation and application of law needs to use some common sense, we can imagine the introduction of the empirical science will impact the world view of legal dogmatics. For example, when the constitutionalism optimistically emphasizes the contribution by the protection of constitutional rights, the detached sociology will point out the rapid raise of social inequality in wealth and the difference of filfulling the function of constitutional rights due to the structure of the social hierarchy, and it will even emphasize low proportion of constitutional lawsuits.

Another kind of "co-operation" may offer even more radical critiques on legal dogmatics. We can call it critique of ideology on law, whether it emerged from the Left, the new Left, or various critical legal studies that emerged after the 1970's, such as feminist jurisprudence, critical racial movement, and postcolonial jurisprudence. They all strongly challenge and criticize the implied presuppositions in mainstream jurisprudence. What they contribute to the legal dogmatics may be not the construction, but rather a radical challenge. However, in a long-term, they will force jurisprudence to face the social reality, which is the reality regulated and presupposed by the law, though more radically.

IV. Conclusion

In recent years, more attention has been paid to interdisciplinary studies of law. An interdisciplinary study in law means the study of law by means of another scientific approach, other than traditional legal analysis. This seems to imply somehow the deficiency of the traditional legal studies. For the communities of legal studies, legal investigation through other approaches can expand the vision of the field, even bringing some reflection on the basic prerequisite of legal science. The problem is, what influence can these so called interdisciplinary studies in law bring to legal science? Can their research results be "absorbed" by legal science? How can legal science make use of them? A critical point will be the relationship between legal science and interdisciplinary studies.

In order to ascertain the relations between these different kinds of knowledge, it is necessary to investigate the nature of legal knowledge. This article asserts that the true nature of legal science is doctrinal (dogmatic), which is necessary to specify the relationship of legal science to legal dogmatics and to justify why it is legal dogmatics.

The knowledge interest of legal dogmatics is to obtain the normative meaning of legal text. It uses hermeneutics as its method to fulfill the task. The other sciences, especially social sciences, observe the social fact as empirical reality. They try to explain the social reality. The reality of law as object of investigation has different meaning for legal science and social sciences. There are alternative relationships between these two kinds of science. One aims to integrate the outcomes of interdisciplinary studies into legal dogmatics. The other aims to integrate doctrinal knowledge of law into, for example, social sciences.

In order to find an entrance for social science into legal dogmatics, the construction of doctrinal knowledge must be decomposed. This can be achieved through the analysis of the forms of legal argumentation. Since the teleological argument, especially in the form of consequential argument, involves both normative and cognitive (empirical) elements, it is an appropriate place for the "integration". It must be clarified that an empirical argument is not only related to an empirical statement, it also includes the theoretical perspective implied in it. The consequential argument has for this reason connection with a theoretical dimension in the social science. Consequently it opens some ways to the empirical studies. The needs for legal dogmatics to engage with social sciences take place here.

There is another possible relationship between legal dogmatics and interdisciplinary studies: a non-integrative, critical one. Since legal dogmatics often makes use of common sense by interpreting the law, the insights offered by empirical sciences that are critical can be deconstructive to legal science. It can be contributive to challenge its background assumptions that are often decisive in legal decision making.

Convergence of Legal Methodology and Philosophy of Science: The Fusion of Fact and Law[*]

Thomas Weishing Huang

I. Introduction

Although there has been growing awareness that the dichotomy between fact and law is untenable, legal scholars and practicing lawyers continue to accept as true that fact and law are, or could be regarded as, fundamentally different.

Treatises on legal methodology continue to emphasize or pay lip services to the distinction and characterize the solution of legal problems simply as legal syllogisms. In other words, it is a process under which legal rules become the major premises, and facts are treated as minor premises. The results, then, are conclusions of simple operation of syllogisms. Whereas the determination of facts is largely regarded as unproblematic and simply as the task of careful observations and painstaking collection

---

[*] The author wishes to acknowledge a generous financial grant from Shih-Hsin University for the research of this paper.

of data, the application of law is, at the most, a matter of a proper application using sound interpretative methods.

In practice, it is axiomatic, at least under Anglo-American law, that the fact is for the jury (where the right is not waived), and the law is for the court. In many civil law countries, appeals from the lower court decisions are frequently restricted to a review of issues of law.[1] In many constitutions under which the judicial review is centralized in the constitutional court, a distinction is made between abstract and concrete reviews.[2] In US Federal Rules of Evidence, adjudicative facts are differentiated from "legislative" ones.[3]

It is not, to be sure, that no one has ever questioned until recently the adequacy of this dualistic view of fact and law. The criticisms, however, almost always stop short of refuting any essential differences in fact and law and do not carry the arguments to their logical conclusions. Karl Llewellyn, for example, maintained that one tends to see what one believes or what one wants to see by overlooking what one does not want to see, particularly in categorizing legal facts.[4] He, nevertheless, did not hold that to know fact and law means the same thing.

I argue that

(1) The legal application as an operation of a logical syllogism is a myth.

(2) Acceptance of judicial syllogisms obscures the importance of "fact" in the legal application.

(3) There is no inherent difference between fact and law, fact and theory, fact and value.

---

[1] Under the French legal system for example, cases referred to Courde cassation or appeals to Conseil d'État are limited to reviews of points of law. See Catherine Elliott & Catherine Vernon, *French Legal System*, 2000, pp. 139,190. Similarly, ordinary appeals at the second instance (revision) under German civil procedure review only points of law. Nigel Foster & Satish Sule, *German Legal System and Laws*, 3d ed. 2002, p. 134.

[2] See *infra* note 25 and the accompanying texts.

[3] See *infra* note 22 and the accompanying texts.

[4] Karl N. Llewellyn, *The Case Law System in America*, Paul Gewirtz ed., Michael Ansaldi trans., 1985, p. 39. ("A lawyer has no wish to deal with isolated facts, with the Unique. He wants to deal with acts as instances of fact *categories*. Within the raw factual matter, he seeks out the few "essential" facts, those which are of legal significance because they fit into a legal fact category, thus providing a handle for "applying" a legal rule.... [W]e are apt to slip into the belief that not only is there generally just one possible way to classify facts, but also that *the particular classification made* in a specific lawsuit has something necessary, something foreordained about it.") (Emphasis original).

(4) The widely-held view that the method of research in social sciences (including law) is far inferior to that of natural sciences [5] and that the former has a great distance to catch up with the latter is historically incorrect.[6]

(5) We do not find, but construct, facts (and of course law).

(6) The division between the different tasks for the jury and the court, adjudicative and legislative facts, reviews of facts and reviews of law, as well as abstract and concrete reviews is based on the faulty distinction between fact and law. Once this basic dichotomy is abandoned, all the above distinctions become untenable.

II. The Dichotomy between Fact and Law

1. The Determination of Fact and the Application of Law

One of the most entrenched notions in law consists of the belief that the application of law entails finding of facts and then applying laws, using proper interpretative methods, to these facts. The solutions come more or less naturally out of this process. Basically, this equals to the operation as syllogisms in logic. This belief becomes so prevalent as the "science of law" movement resulted in massive codification in continental Europe. The problem of law or legal application is essentially the logical operation of syllogisms in which the law becomes the major premise and the finding of facts

---

[5] John Stuart Mill, Logic, Ratiocination and Inductive: BKS IV-VI, in 8 *Collected Works of John Stuart Mill*, J. M. Robson ed., [1974]2006, p. 833.

[6] See generally John Henry, *The Scientific Revolution and the Origins of Modern Science*, 3d ed., 2008, p. 102. (discussing Bacon, Boyle, and the Royal Society and the similarity between their views of scientific methods and the legal process). See also Steven Shapin, *A Social History of Truth: Civility and Science in Seventeenth-Century England*, 1994, p. 214. ([W]riters sometimes traced analogies with formal legal procedures. Sprat noted that people were generally content that the law condemn persons on the agreeing testimony of "two, or three witnesses", and urged that they be equally content in assenting to knowledge-claims "if they have the concurring Testimonies of *threescore or on hundred*" fellows of the Royal Society. Boyle fleshed out his apology for moral certainty by drawing attention to "the practice of our courts of justice here in England" in cases of murder "and some other criminal causes"); Barbara J. Shapiro, *Beyond Reasonable Doubt and Probable Cause: Historical Perspectives on The Anglo-American Law of Evidence*, 1991, p. 34 ("Although Gambier's Guide is not a legal treaties, its assumptions about the nature of knowledge and the way one should reach judgment in matters of fact were relevant to the legal community. The overlap between the legal and nonlegal work is often so great that it is difficult to know which should be labeled "legal" and which should not. What is clear, however, is that the growing treatise literature on the law of evidence participated in broader intellectual currents and shared rather widely held views on the nature of evidence and proof".)

is treated as the minor premise. The court would then simply deduce legal solutions from these premises.[7] Traditional legal reasoning and most of the judicial decisions in France hold until to date the same formalistic views and practices, and dubs the process as "syllogisme judiciaire".[8] This is also reflected in the succinct manner in which French courts render their decisions. Similarly, legal formalism or legalism under Anglo-American law fares no better than believing that "[t]he ideal legalist decision is the product of a syllogism in which a rule of law supplies the major premise, the facts of the case supply the minor one, and the decision is the conclusion".[9]

Traditionally, scholars may realize the difficulties in figuring out what legal facts are, they, however, do not question the distinction between fact and law. Again, Llewellyn readily acknowledged the difficulty in the determination of facts, but only hinted the indirect influence of legal categories (legal theories) on categorizing facts.[10]

However, on careful reflection, lawyers must admit that we do not actually obtain legal solutions from syllogisms. As John Dewey already stated long time ago: "Logical forms such as one finds in a logical treatise do not pretend to tell how we think or even how we should think. No one ever arrived at the idea that Socrates, or any other creature, was mortal by following the form of the syllogism."[11] If, however, one has arrived at that notion by gathering and interpreting evidence and wishes to expound to another person the reasons of his belief, no one, of course, has any objection to his using the syllogistic form for presenting the argument in its most compact form.

---

[7] Geoffrey Samuel, *Epistemology and Method In Law*, 2003, p. 29.

[8] Eva Steiner, *French Legal Method*, 2002, p. 131.

[9] Richard A. Posner, *How Judges Think*, 2008, p. 41. A typical treatment of legal reasoning as a deductive process and consider a "finding of fact" only a matter of proof, see e. g. Neil MacCormick, *Legal Reasoning and Legal Theory*, 1978, pp. 86—97.

[10] Llewellyn, *The Case Law System in America*, pp. 53—54. ("[A] fact situation admits of more than one of the constructions espoused; that *each* way of construing the facts will contain a degree of violence to either the fact situation or the classifying category. For the facts will typically require the making of some "adjustments" to a category which, before the court came to construe these facts, was not *quite* applicable to them. There is a slight shifting of either the facts or the category, and neither competing interpretation is "right" or "wrong." Rather, the interpretation either does or does not further a particular purpose, the interpreter tacitly choosing from among various possible purposes (such as practicality of the solution in the real world, maintaining balance in the legal system, etc.") (Emphasis original).

[11] John Dewey, *How We Think* (Emphasis original), 1933, p. 74.

If using syllogisms is not what the reality of the applications of law, what then actually takes place? Judge Posner believes that judges, particularly those sit in the appellate courts, rely on intuition, rather than logic, in deciding cases.[12] This is, of course, not the same as saying that once a certain conclusion has been reached by judges, the decisions could not be presented, as after-thoughts, in syllogisms. He went on to observe that

> Judges cast a great many votes in the course of a year and do not have time to engage in elaborate analytical procedures before each vote is cast, or afterward for that matter. Typically, appellate judges read the briefs in advance of oral argument; discuss the case with their law clerks, also in advance; listen to the argument; and afterward, usually right afterward, discuss the case briefly with their colleagues and take a vote that is tentative but usually turns out to be final. At every stage the judge's reasoning process is primarily intuitive.[13]

The reason that legal methodologists continue to pay lip services to the operation of legal syllogisms and believe the method to be true and useful can only be explained by another keen observation. Dewey again said:

> The history of scientific beliefs also shows that when a wrong theory once gets general acceptance, men will expend ingenuity of thought in buttressing it with additional errors rather than surrender it and start in a new direction; witness for example the elaborate pains taken to preserve the Ptolemaic theory of the solar system. Even today correct multitude merely because they are current and popular rather than because the multitude understands the reasons upon which they rest.[14]

This is exactly the situation with the legal syllogism. No lawyer ever thinks that way for reaching legal solutions. It is not even necessary that the presentation of legal arguments be arranged to look like syllogisms. Yet methodologists continue to maintain that legal applications involve two distinctive categories of fact and law, as well as two separate processes of finding the objective fact (truth) and making correct legal interpretations. I have argued so far that the process as logical syllogisms has

---

[12] Posner, *How Judges Think*, p. 110.
[13] Ibid.
[14] Dewey, *How We Think*, p. 24.

never taken place except maybe as after thoughts, and will show that the distinction between fact and law can never be meaningfully drawn.

2. The Fact for the Jury and the Law for the Judge

It is a well known practice in Anglo-American law that the issues of fact are for the jury (if the right is not waived) and those of law are for the judge. Under these practices, factual questions had to be strictly separated from legal questions, so a juror would address only those questions within his competence. What the jury then found about a question of fact, however, was fixed once and for all for the remainder of the proceedings. In criminal proceedings, for example, the jury's not-guilty verdict binds the court and will entitle the defendant to be released right on the spot. Questions of fact decided by the jury, then, could not be appealed; only questions of law could.[15]

Although it is widely assumed that the jury/judge distinction is particular under the Anglo-American legal system, it is historically incorrect to attribute the jury system exclusively to that system. In the early Republic period in the Roman Empire, in addition to magistrates who handled legal proceedings, a single juror (called index) was selected among citizens to hear arguments of facts.[16] Therefore, even in the civil law tradition, the jury system was not entirely unknown.

As far as Anglo-American law is concern, the jury/judge dichotomy is vastly exaggerated. In reality, practically all doctrinal or historical facts have never been submitted to the jury for evaluation.[17] Rather, those facts are decided by judges without any involvement of the jury. In addition, it is quite arbitrary in dividing what are facts for the jury. For example, whereas the US Uniform Commercial Code prescribes that the issue of conscionability in sales is for the court to decide[18], the question of good faith, nevertheless, is usually treated as an issue of law for the court.[19] Obviously, it is difficult to discern objective criteria for making such a dis-

---

[15] Llewellyn, *The Case Law System in America*, p. 34.
[16] Peter Stein, *Roman Law In European History*, 1999, pp. 4—5, p. 9.
[17] David L. Faigman, *Constitutional Fiction: A Unified Theory of Constitutional Facts*, 2008, p. 119.
[18] Ali, *Uniform Commercial Code: 1962 Official Text with Comment*, § 2-302 (2) (1963) ("The commercial evidence referred to in subsection (2) is for the court's consideration, not the jury's").
[19] *See* Market Street Associates v. Frey, 941 F. 2d. 588 (7th Cir. 1991).

tinction.

One of the reasons that the fact/law distinction must be made lies in the fact that the Constitution of the United States requires such difference to be drawn. Its seventh amendment provides that

> In suits at common law...the right of trial by jury shall be preserved, and no fact tried by a jury, shall be otherwise re-examined in any Court of the United States, than according to the rule of the common law.[20]

Nevertheless, this distinction under the influence of common law and the requirement of the Constitution can hardly provide proof for the essential differences between fact and law. They only require, for practical and constitutional purposes, that a distinction be made in law practice. Therefore, scholars who have studies this fact/law dichotomy conclude that such distinction represent less of any inherent difference between the two than of a convention maintained by tradition and practical considerations.[21]

3. Adjudicative v. Legislative Facts

According to US Federal Rules of Evidence, its Rule 201 deals only with facts that are relevant to the issue or issues of the case, which the rule terms "adjudicative" facts. It does not deal with so-called "legislative" facts, which, broadly speaking, constitute the factual framework for the intellectual apparatus of a thinking person.[22]

However, the term "legislative" is somewhat misleading. While adjudicative facts are simply the facts of the particular case, "legislative" facts, on the other hand, are those which have relevance to legal reasoning and the lawmaking process, whether in the formulation of a legal principle or ruling by a judge or court or in the enactment of a legislative body.[23] In other words, "legislative" facts are nothing but what traditionally being categorized as social conditions and legal theories.

The theoretical nature of "legislative" facts can also be shown by the fact that

---

[20] U.S. Const. Amend. VII.
[21] Gary Lawson, "Legal Theory: Proving the Law", 86 *NW. U. L. REV.* 863 (1992).
[22] Moore's *Federal Practice*, 1983 Rules Pamphlet: *Federal Rules of Evidence*, Matthew Bender ed., 1983, Part 2, p.36.
[23] Ibid., p.37.

as well as adjudicative facts are subject to federal rules of evidence, these rules do not provide guidance for recognizing "legislative facts".[24] For all we know, one might as well call "legislative facts" "legislative theories".

Similar to the above distinction is the attempt to separate concrete reviews from the so-called abstract constitutional reviews.[25] While the former deals with concrete facts of the case, the latter is supposed to construct law without any reference to the factual background from which the abstract review becomes necessary. Again, facts are thought to be different from law.

III. The Dichotomy between Fact and Theories

1. Objective Reality

The source of the dichotomy between fact and law comes from another influential dualistic view of creating and treating theories and realities (facts) as different. From this distinction, it is only a small step to differentiate between facts and theories based on the traditional Western idea of the existence of objective realities in the world. The view on objective realities could be traced back, if not to Parmenides [26], at least to Plato. It was Plato who conceived of an existence of a reality in this world called the Form. According to him, the pursuit of knowledge and truth is to attempt to know this objective reality called the Form [27], even though we may only succeed in knowing its appearance. This notion was further developed by Descartes who drew distinction between body and mind, subject and object, and turned those dualistic views into one of the most dominant thoughts in the Western intellectual history.

Based on this concept of an objective reality, facts represent the reality and are supposed to correspond to it as well. Facts, therefore, are meant to be objective in the sense that they are at once independent in existence and accurately represent the

---

[24] Dean M. Hashimoto, "Science as Mythology in Constitutional Law", 76 OR. L. REV., p. 120 (1997).

[25] Foster, German Legal System and Laws, p. 241.

[26] See 2 W. K. C. Guthrie, A History of Greek Philosophy: The Presocratic Tradition from Parmenidies to Democritus, 1965, p. 4.

[27] Plato, Parmenides, in The Collected Dialogues, Including the Letters, Hamilton and Huntington Cairns eds., 1961, pp. 928—929.

reality. Accordingly, factual statements are faithful descriptions of these objectively independent facts and they are themselves objective. In the same vein, legal facts could only represent objective description of legal events.

This dualistic view has been severely criticized by many modern philosophers for a long time.[28] Hilary Putnam once criticized these views and stated:

> What of the idea that right description of the world is the same thing as "objectivity"? This idea rests, pretty dearly, on the supposition that "objectivity" means correspondence to objects (an idea that corresponds to the etymology of the word, of course). But it is not only normative truths such as "Murder is wrong" that pose counterexamples to this idea; as 1 argue elsewhere, mathematical and logic truth are likewise examples of "objectivity without objects". To be sure, many philosophers tell us that we have to posit peculiar objects (so-called abstract entities) to account for mathematical truth; but this does not help at all, as we can see by asking, "Would mathematics work one bit less well if these funny objects stopped existing?" Those who posit "abstract entities" to account for the success of mathematics do not claim that we (or any other things in the empirical world) interact with the abstract entities. But if any entities do not interact with us or with the empirical world at all, then doesn't it follow that everything would be the same if they didn't exist?[29]

In addition, not only facts do not correspond to (non-existent) independent objects, they are socially constructed according to the prevailing collective thought. They are true in the sense not because they accurately represent the objective reality, but because they are intersubjectively accepted as true by a particular community.

In a previously unknown book on development of scientific facts made popular by philosophers like Thomas Kuhn, Ludwik Fleck stressed the importance of the social aspect of science. Scholars summarized Ludwik Fleck's observations and stated that

> Truth in science is a function of the particular style of thinking that has been accepted by the thought collective. To be correct is rather to be accepted. Thus truth can vary with time and culture, for it is determined by a

---

[28] See generally Richard Rorty, *Philosophy and the Mirror of Nature*, 1979, particularly chs. 3 & 4.
[29] Hilary Putnam, *The Collapse of the Fact/Value Dichotomy and Other Essays*, 2002, p. 33.

simple correspondence theory of truth relating words to objects or cognition to facts. There is no objective and absolute truth. Truth is rather a stylized solution which is unique and singular only with respect to a particular thought style. It is not so much subjective as intersubjective or collective. And although relative it is not arbitrary, since it is a function of thought style.[30]

Obviously, people who hold strong version of realism will not agree with the above statements. Alvin Goldman, for example, criticized the holistic and postmodern thought and continued to maintain the existence and usefulness of such an objective reality. Goldman likened scientific facts as photographic images and stated that

> Certain types of scientific data...are photographs or instrument printouts that can be examined by observers quite leisurely and circumspectly. Needless to say, scientists with different theoretical beliefs may still disagree about the disputed causes of observed marks, tracks, or features in photographs or printouts they examine. But in terms of more primitive, less contentious, types of descriptions of these observable objects, there can be extensive agreement and accuracy.[31]

He further stated that

> ...since knowledge is true belief, knowledge also involves truth; and what is true, as we have seen, is not a human construct as opposed to being of the world....Knowledge partly consists of belief, and belief is always local or situated because it is always the belief of a particular knower or group of knowers who live at particular points in time. But knowledge also partly consists of truth, and when a fully determinate proposition is true, it is true for all time, not just at particular times or places. The proposition that there is a cup on the kitchen table at such-and-such an address at noon, Greenwich Mean Time, October 18,1997,is either timelessly true or timelessly false.[32]

But to remain timelessly true, these examples and conclusions derive neither from direct observation nor from personal experience. If we rule out sheer fantasies or

---

[30] Ludwik Fleck, *Genesis And Development of a Scientific Fact*, Thaddeus J. Trenn & Robert K. Merton eds., 1977(Editors' descriptive analysis), p.156.
[31] Alvin I. Goldman, *Knowledge in A Social World*, 1999, p.241.
[32] Ibid., p.21.

reflections as sources of reliable knowledge, Alvin Goldman can make his claims only because many people would intersubjectively agree that his examples may be true. In other words, we either have socially construed them as true or simply have all practiced them.[33] The very meaning of truth is, therefore, conventional.

For these reasons, some modern philosophers, who believe that empiricism is over rated, frequently criticize the theory that objective facts can be obtained though experiments and observations. Nelson Goodman, for example, held that

> The perceptual is no more a rather distorted version of the physical facts than the physical is a highly artificial version of the perceptual facts. If we are tempted to say that "both are versions of the same facts", this must no more be taken to imply that there independent facts of which both are versions than likeness of meaning between two terms implies that there are some entities called meanings. "Fact" like "meaning" is a syncategorematic term; for facts, after all, are obviously factitious.[34]

Goodman further criticized fundationalists and accused them of believing that "facts are found not made, that facts constitute the one and the only world, and that knowledge consists of believing the facts".[35] He lamented that these articles of faith so blind most of us and distort our views that "fabrication of fact" has a paradoxical sound. "Fabrication" has become a synonym for "falsehood" or "fiction" as contrasted with "truth" or "fact".[36]

2. Facts Are Theory-Laden

Norwood Hanson, who single-handed made popular the term "theory-laden" of observations or facts, refused to draw sharp distinction between facts and theories. Just like his teacher Ludwig Wittgenstein, Hanson maintained that, for practical purposes, the game of chess is one and the same as its rules. So he wrote:

---

[33] Ludwig Wittgenstein, *Philosophical Investigations* § 241, 3d ed., 1958. ("So you are saying that human agreement decides what is true and what is false?"—It is what human beings *say* that is true and false; and they agree in the *language* they use. That is not agreement in opinions but in form of life.) (Emphasis original).

[34] Nelson Goodman, *Ways of World Making*, 1978, pp. 92—93.

[35] Ibid., p. 91.

[36] Ibid.

The view thus arises that "the facts" are just those conditions a subject matter meets such that a given theory might be applied to it—the boundary conditions. In that sense "the facts are theoretically determined somewhat as the rules of chess determine what layout the chessboard must have at the onset, and what moves will be permissible therefrom so that the subsequent interchange could be describable as chess".[37]

The most obvious proof that facts and law are inseparable and are essentially the same lie in the fact that one can even describe "legal facts." Without law, i. e. legal theories, there can never be any legal facts, that is, if one insists on calling them "facts". It is, therefore, extraordinary to maintain that facts and law are two distinct categories. In reality, to construct legal facts is nothing but a particular way of constructing legal theories.

In an old common law case dealing with the concept of anticipatory breach in contract law, the court allowed the promisee to sue the employer for breach of contract way before the actual date of the employment previously agreed upon.[38] On the other hand, a U.S. Court of Appeal ruled that a sub-contractor's indication of difficulty in obtaining necessary materials for the project and of his inability to perform on time did not justify plaintiff's insecurity and the law suit prior to the agreed date for the completion of the contract.[39] The differences in recognizing the fact of insecurity on the part of the plaintiffs in those two cases can only be explained in the different understanding of the legal theories by the two courts.

More recently, settlement of the issue of separation of State and church, or the establishment of a religion concerning the first amendment of the US Constitution entangled with the nature of the creation-science as depicted in the Bible (biblical facts).[40] The treatment of biblical facts and the disposition of the case depended to a great extent on the court's acceptance of what science is supposed to be. Therefore, the court's "finding" (construction in reality) of "facts" is indistinguishable

---

[37] Norwood R. Hanson, *Patterns of Discovery*, 1969, p. 12.

[38] Hochster v. De La Tour, (1853) 118 Eng. Rep. 922 (Q. B.), in E. Allan Farnsworth, William F. Young, Carol Sanger, *Contracts: Cases and Materials*, 6th ed., 2001, p. 741.

[39] *See* mccloskey & Co. V. Minweld Steel Co., 220 F. 2d 101 (3d Cir. 1955).

[40] mclean v. Arkansas Board of Education, 29 F. Supp. 1255 (E. D. Ark. 1982). For discussions and debates on demarcation between science and pseudo-science in conjunction with this case, *see* Martin Curd & J. S. Cover, *Philosophy of Science: The Central Issues*, 1998, pp. 38—53, pp. 74—77.

from theoretical construction and exposition of the nature of science.

Additional proof of the theoretical nature of facts can be provided by what most people believe to be the most neutral and objective facts, namely, numbers and figures. We frequently heard that "numbers don't lie" or "numbers speak for themselves", as if once facts are represented in numbers, they become indisputable truth. The reality is far from this naïve preconception, as obviously random numbers do not make sense and the fact represented by statistical figures depends on statistical theories and the fact contained in financial and accounting statements count on accounting theories to be understood.[41]

Facts are so theory-laden that they are indistinguishable from theories. "Could '$E = MC^2$' have expressed a fact a million years ago' For whom?"[42] asked Hanson. Obvious not until we (i.e. Albert Einstein) invented that theory to describe the fact.

3. Statements of Facts

Factual events are not "facts". They are not even comprehensible to most of us who did not partake in direct observations. Indescribable events, therefore, cannot become facts. Hanson once wrote:

> What would an inexpressible fact be like? Not a complicated, incompletely understood fact, but one "inexpressible in principle", a fact which constitutionally resists articulation? When would we be referred to a fact with the aside that it must always elude linguistic expression? To what would we have been directed? Unknown facts of course elude expression....Could one know facts for which no expression was available, and what sense is there in even speaking of unknowable facts?[43]

In other words, we come to know facts only through statements of facts. In reality, we may say that we know only statements of facts and nothing more.

According to some sociologists, there is a certain procedure under which statements of facts are constructed. Dorothy Smith stated rhetorically that

---

[41] For accounting, see Mary Poovey, *A History of the Modern Fact: Problems of Knowledge in the Sciences of Wealth and Society* xvi, 1998, p.29.

[42] Norwood R. Hanson, *Observation & Explanation: A Guide to Philosophy of Science*, 1971, p.15.

[43] Hanson, *Patterns of Discovery*, p.31.

> The actual events are not facts. It is the use of proper procedure for categorizing events which transforms them into facts. A fact is something that is already categorized, already worked up to conform to the model of what the fact should be like. To describe something as a fact or to treat something as a fact implies that the events themselves—what happened—entitled or authorize the teller of the tale to treat that categorization as ineluctable. Whether I wish it or not, it is a fact.[44]

Therefore, facts are factual statements given by persons of certain competence for giving such statements (such as witnesses or experts) according to pre-existing categories and preconceptions. It, therefore, would not be far from the truth in stating that statements of facts are particular types of theoretical statements.

We may recall Goldman's statements that facts are objective in the sense that they could be photographic representation of realities.[45] Considering from linguistic points of view, that belief ignores statements of facts and is far from being accurate. Therefore Hanson stated that

> Not all the elements of statement correspond to the elements of pictures: only someone who misunderstood the uses of language would expect otherwise. There is a "linguistic" factor in seeing, although there is nothing linguistic about what forms in the eye, or in the mind's eye. Unless there were this linguistic element, nothing we ever observed could have relevance for our knowledge.[46]

Rather, "the fact" emerge here as the world's possibilities for being described in some available language—which possibilities will be every bit as "theory-laden" as the descriptions themselves are disclosed to be.

Even a self-proclaimed "constructive empiricist" like Bas Fraassen[47] does not doubt that statements of facts are theory-laden. He said that

> All our language is thoroughly theory-infected. If we could cleanse our language of theory-laden terms...we would end up with nothing useful. The way

---

[44] Dorothy E. Smith, *Texts, Facts, and Femininity: Exploring the Relations of Rules*, 1990, p. 27.
[45] Goldman, *Knowledge in A Social World*, and the accompanying texts.
[46] Hanson, *Patterns of Discovery*, p. 25.
[47] Very roughly, Fraassen believes that scientific theories can be accepted without endorsing their being true, as long as theories are empirically adequate. *See* Bas C. Van Fraassen, *The Scientific Image*, 1980, pp. 23—25.

we talk, and scientists talk, is guided by the pictures provided by previously accepted theories. This is true also...of experimental reports. Hygienic reconstructions of language such as the positivists envisaged are simply not on.[48]

It is the same with John Searle who is a linguist and who also happens to be a strong realist. He admits at least some facts are language dependent and when the language elements are gone so are the facts.[49]

Therefore, facts and theories are separated as if they are two different categories solely for conventional reasons. Without theories, facts could not be constructed; taken away theories from statements of facts, one takes away, not only theories, but also facts.

IV. The Dichotomy between Fact and Values

Scholars usually attributed the thesis that normative propositions could not be logically deduced from descriptive ones to David Hume. In one of his obscure statements, he once wrote that

> In every system of morality, which I have hitherto met with, I have always remarked, that the author proceeds for some time in the ordinary way of reasoning, and establishes the being of a God, or makes observations concerning human affairs; when of a sudden I am surprised to find, that instead of the usual copulations of propositions, Is, and is not, I meet with no proposition that is not connected with an ought, or an ought not. This change is imperceptible; but is, however, of the last consequence. For it is as this ought, or ought not, expresses some new relation or affirmation, it Is necessary that it should be observed and explained; and at the same that a reason should be given, for what seems altogether inconceivable, how this new relation can be a deduction from others, which are entirely different from it.[50]

On close examination, he did not, however, exactly maintain the view that no normative propositions could ever be logically deduced from descriptive ones. What

---

[48] Ibid., p. 14.
[49] John R. Searle, *The Construction of Social Reality*, 1995, p. 61.
[50] David Hume, *A Treaty of Human Nature*, nuvision ed. 2007, p. 335.

he did say was that they represent two different relationships and ought to be explained as to how one could be derived from the other.

According to Hilary Putnam, a philosophical view may gradually come to be accepted by many people as if it were common sense. Some may be developed into very sophisticated theories like statements of "fact" are capable of being "objectively true" and are capable of being "objectively warranted". On the other hand, "value judgment, according to the most extreme proponents of a sharp 'fact/value' dichotomy, are completely outside the sphere of reason".[51]

Putnam rejected, however, the dichotomy of facts and values and wrote

> The example of the predicate "cruel" also suggests that the problem is not just that the empiricist's (and later the logical positivist's) notion of a "fact" was much too narrow from the start. A deeper problem is that, from Hume on, empiricists—and not only empiricists but many others as well, in and outside of philosophy—failed to appreciate the ways in which factual description and valuation can and must be entangled.[52]

He further argued that

> ...."every fact is value loaded and every one of our values loads some fact". The argument in a nutshell was that fact (or truth) and rationality are interdependent notions. A fact is something that it is rational to believe, or, more precisely, the notion of a fact (or a true statement) is an idealization of the notion of a statement that it is rational to believe....The decision that a picture of the world is true (or true by our present lights, or "as true as anything is") and answers the relevant questions (as well as we are able to answer them) rests on and reveals our total system of value commitments. A being with no values would have no facts either.[53]

In addition, since we inevitably observe or understand the world (facts) through our preconceptions or pre-understandings shaped by our traditions[54], the facts so constructed can only be as value-affected as they are theory-laden. There-

---

[51] Hilary Putnam, *The Collapse of the Fact/Value Dichotomy and Other Essays*, 2002, p.1.
[52] Ibid., pp.26—27.
[53] Hilary Putnam, *Reason, Truth and History*, 1981, p.201.
[54] See generally Hans Gadamer, *Truth and Method*, J. Weinsheimer & D. Marshall trans., 2d ed., 1988.

fore, to proceed with value-neutral observation and understanding of facts is to proceed with no observation or understanding of this world at all.

My rejection of the fact/value distinction obviously raises a whole host of issues beyond the scope of the discussion of this paper which has a more modest aim of pointing out only the value-ladenness of facts. On the other hand, it suffices to say that the traditional view regarding law as a system of norms not only tends to ignore non-normative elements (such as causation for example) according to its own definition, but also draws a untenable sharp line between fact and value in law.

V. Where Do Facts Come From?

1. What Are Facts?

To some positivists like Émile Durkheim, it is not only possible, but also important to treat a (social) fact as a thing (une chose). To Durkheim, a fact is something that we know from without compared to something that which we know from within. Once we treat a social fact as a thing we will be able to be objective as things are themselves objective.[55]

David Hume, on the other hand, considered the so-called fact nothing but an impression created by sensation in our mind. In a famous passage, he asked rhetorically:

> Where is that mater of fact that we call crime; point it out; determine the time of its existence; describe its essence or nature; explain the sense or faculty to which it discovers itself. It resides in the mind of the person who is ungrateful. He must, therefore, fell it and be conscious of it. But nothing is there except the passion of ill will or of absolute indifference. You cannot say that these, of themselves, always, and in all circumstances, are crimes. No, they are only crimes when directed towards persons who have before expressed and displayed good-will towards us. Consequently, complication of circumstances which being presented to the spectator excites the sentiment of blame, by the particular structure and fabric of his mind.[56]

---

[55] Émile Durkheim, *Les Régles De La Mèthode SociologiqueFlammarion* ed. ,1977, p. 77.
[56] David Hume, *Enquires Concerning Human Understanding and Concerning the Principles of Morals*, 3d rev. Ed. 1975(Emphasis original), p. 287.

Therefore, Hume did not believe there existed independent realities called facts. This leads to another issue as to whether facts correspond to independent realities alluded to previously.

But social realities are not objective things, but just collective social beliefs. Social reality contains elements of beliefs and convictions which are real because they are so defined by the participants and which escape sensory observation. "To the inhabitants of Salem in the seventeenth century, witchcraft was not a delusion but an element of their social reality and is as such open to investigation by the social scientist."[57]

Precisely because facts and realities are socially constructed, facts and the appearance of the independent realities are the end product of the same process and comes from the same source. No wonder scientists marvel at the "accuracy" of their discoveries with the objective realities.[58] Thus, the traditional way of thinking from observation to finding of facts is reversed. Applying this theory to law, one does not find pre-exiting legal facts. Rather, one constructs legal facts and legal events to which the former is supposed to represent.

Historically, "facts" were things which required proofs to become true or reliable. According to Barbara Sharpiro,

> Some matters of fact might be considered "proved" and others doubtful or false. "Fact" in this context did not necessarily refer to an established truth but often to an issue of truth. Indeed, one of the great changes that occurred over the course of two centuries in some cultural arenas was the transformation of "fact" from something that had to be sufficiently proved by appropriate evidence to be considered worthy of belief to something for which appropriate verification had already taken place.[59]

Today, one frequently asserts that "It is a fact!" or "It is an indisputable fact!" to try to win the argument. How one goes about proving a scientific or legal fact is the subject of discussion in the following two sections.

---

[57] 1 Alfred Schutz, *Collected Papers: The Problems of Social Reality*, Maurice Natanson ed., 1962, p. 54.

[58] Bruno Latour And Steve Woolgar, *Laboratory Life: The Construction of Scientific Facts*, 1986, p. 183.

[59] Barbara J. Shapiro, *A Culture of Fact: England, 1550—1720*, p. 31 (2000).

2. Scientific Facts

(1) Observations and their Limitations

Francis Bacon is considered a towering figure in the history of science in no small measure for his commitment to observation and experimentation as reliable scientific methods.[60] From then on, scientific investigations entail simply collection of sufficient data and careful analysis of those data by any scientist to derive facts either to confirm or refute theories (hypotheses).[61]

Ludwig Fleck, however, questioned this established view of the development of scientific facts. According to him, scientists almost always stumble into materials that they will use. Whether and how they will use those materials depend on their psychological propensity which more or less fixed by their professional habits determined by collective thought types of the community. While his initial observations offer him only chaos, as he persists and muddles along, he begins to "see" or "experience" things. Eventually "what has been revealed and conceptually summarized in a scientific statement is an artificial structure, related but only genetically so, both to the original intention and to the substance of the "first" observation. The original observation K need not even belong to the same class as that of the facts it led J toward."[62] Fleck, therefore, not only deny the existence of an objective world "out there" simply waiting to be discovered by any scientist, but also pointed out the theory-ladenness of observations and their social characteristics.

Hanson also confirmed that it is useless to accumulate materials or data without theories to guide them and make them understandable. In one of his famous points, he stated: "Being able to make sense of the sensors requires knowledge and theory—not simply more sense signals. (Understanding the significance of the signal flags fluttering from the bridge of the Queen Elizabeth does not usually require still more flags to be flown!)."[63]

Similarly, Hanson stated in another place that

---

[60] Steve Shapin, *The Scientific Revolution*, 1996, pp. 92—94.
[61] Curd & Cover, *Philosophy of Science: The Central Issues*, p. 355.
[62] Fleck, *Genesis And Development of a Scientific Fact*, p. 89 (Emphasis added).
[63] Hanson, *Observation & Explanation: A Guide to Philosophy of Science*, p. 5 (Emphasis original).

> Most of us talk of observing facts, looking at them, collecting them, etc. What is observation of a fact? What would one look like? In what could it be collected? I can photograph an object, an event, or even a situation. What would a photograph of a fact be a photograph of? Is a sketch of the dawn a sketch of the fact of which Tycho, Simplicius, Kepler and Galileo were aware? Asking the question suffices. Facts are not picturable, observable entities, seeing the sun on the horizon involves more than soaking up optical sensibilia, we have said; but not so much more that "seeing the fact that the sun is on the horizon" fails to jar the ear.[64]

Even Karl Popper, who is not quite in the same camp as Hanson or Fleck, agreed that both observations and observation statements are always interpretations of facts observed and "they are interpretations in the light of theories".[65] He went even further and said,

> But even the experimenter is not in the main engaged in making exact observations; his work, too, is largely of a theoretical kind. Theory dominates the experimental work from its initial planning up to the finishing touches in the laboratory.[66]

(2) Reports

It is practically impossible for scientists to observe or experiment every thing himself. Therefore, the romantic picture of scientist act as an individualist busy in confirm and refuting every piece fact or theory is largely a myth. Epistemologically, there is no way that any scientist can conduct scientific activities solely on his own without relying on other people's observations or investigations.[67]

Hume was one of the first philosophers to note the importance of testimony. According to him, "there is no species of reasoning more common, more useful, and even necessary to human life, than that which is derived from the testimony of men

---

[64] Hanson, *Patterns of Discovery*, p. 31.
[65] Karl Popper, *The Logic of Scientific Structure*, p. 90, n. 3 ([1959] 2002) (Emphasis original).
[66] Ibid., p. 90.
[67] C. A. J. Coady, *Testimony: A Philosophical Study*, 1992, p. 9. ("Any given scientist, even the most authoritative, will argue from, presuppose, and take for granted numerous observations and experiments that he has not performed for himself. That this is so is obscured by the elements of individualist ideology built into our image of science, the scientist being pictured as utterly self-reliant and self-sufficient, and by the way in which writers tend to refer to 'established' observational and experimental facts as though they themselves had done the observing or experimenting.")

and the reports of eye-witnesses and spectators". [68]

This is why epistemologists believe that "[c]ollaboration is therefore an essential aspect of modern science, and the testimony of fellow workers must be relied upon just as much as your own observations".[69]

A paradox seems to have arisen: On the one hand, the establishment of scientific facts depends on direct observations and experiments; on the other hand, scientist cannot conduct science without relying on other's reports which he did not have opportunity to observe. How does he make sure that the testimony of others and their reports are reliable? Historically, scientists have turned to law for solutions, and this is the subject I turn to next.

3. Legal Facts

It is almost universally agreed that the development of social sciences (including law in my definition) lags far behind that of natural sciences and the former, to reach the same level of maturity as the latter, has a vast distance to catch up. I have already pointed out that John Stuart Mill once observed that the only way for the moral science (today's social sciences) to truly achieve a scientific status was to emulate physics.[70] Historians discovered, however, that this is not an accurate account of the history of science. Barbara Shapiro found that

> During the early modem era the English legal system had produced a well-accepted epistemological framework and a method of implementing it that worked reasonably well in reaching judgments of "fact" necessary to making important social decisions. Much of this epistemology and method could be and was transferred to other sites of knowledge and other knowledge-making situations.[71]

These methods were what previously alluded to, namely, observation and experimentation using a familial legal technique of verifying events in the human world to natural phenomena. In natural history as in law, "matter of fact" could best be es-

---

[68] Quoted in Dan O'Brien, *The Theory of Knowledge*, 2006, p. 51.

[69] Ibid., p. 57.

[70] John Stuart Mill, Logic, Ratiocination And Inductive: BKS IV-VI, in 8 *Collected Works of John Stuart Mill*, p. 895.

[71] Shapiro, *Beyond Reasonable Doubt and Probable Cause: Historical Perspectives on the Anglo-American Law of Evidence*, p. 32.

tablished by the testimony of a sufficient number of firsthand witnesses of appropriate credibility. The term "fact" or "matter of fact" implied, for most of the seventeenth century, not something already worthy of belief or true but rather a matter capable of proof, preferably by multiple eyewitness testimony."[72]

The way Francis Bacon, who was also Lord Chancellor in charge of King's legal affairs, proposed to establish scientific principles is, therefore, strikingly familiar to common law lawyers. Bacon advanced a procedure for finding scientific rules by first making "presentation", then by way of "exclusion and rejection", and making "comparison", tentatively to reach "first harvest". [73] To a common law lawyer, this procedure is analogous to presentation and admission of evidence, and then giving evidence's proper weight to establish a prima facie case in legal procedure. As a matter of fact, Bacon admitted as much that "presentation" was borrowed from the legal concept.[74]

(1) Testimony

Except for jurors of the very early time, judges and jurors are not expected to have first-hand experience of occurred events. However, sound judgments could be arrived at by examining the testimony of those who had seen or heard the events. In order to make such judgments it was necessary to examine the quality and quantity of testimony, to be suspicious of hearsay, and to consider any relevant "circumstances".[75]

Another way of assuring the trust worthiness of testimony was the administering of oaths. Oaths were assumed to enhance the probability of testimonial truth but not to ensure it.[76] As a matter of fact, the assertion that oaths are useful can be traced all the way back to Aristotle, even though he discussed the use of oaths to establish facts in rhetoric, not in law.[77]

---

[72] Ibid., pp. 109—110.
[73] Francis Bacon, *The New Organon*, Lisa Jardine & Michael Silverthorne eds., 2000, pp. 110—136.
[74] Ibid., p. 110, n. 4.
[75] Shapiro, *Beyond Reasonable Doubt and Probable Cause: Historical Perspectives on the Anglo-American Law of Evidence*, p. 31.
[76] Ibid.
[77] Aristotle, Rhetoric To Alexander, In 2 *The Complete Works of Aristotle*, Jonathan Barns ed., 1984, pp. 2283—2290.

(2) Expert Opinions

Similar to scientific reports mentioned previously, construction of facts (called the "finding of fact") must rely on third party's testimony. This is frequently presented in the form of testimony by expert witnesses. The whole category of expert testimony, as we saw earlier, undermines the rather natural idea that reports can be given only to what has been observed (either by the reporter or by someone at the other end of a transmission chain upon whom he eventually relies). Experts do not usually testify to what they have observed, though they may do that too, but rather to an expert view or opinion they may have. The idea is further threatened, or at least subject to modification, by the possibility, which surely exists, of mathematical testimony, since mathematical facts are not in any ordinary way observed.[78]

Although legal procedure originally influenced methodology from the natural sciences for ascertaining scientific fact, one philosopher of science who became fascinated by law found it odd that the present day jury system has many rules and procedures that have little to do with ascertaining truth. He said that he cannot imagine that a scientist, when acts like a juror, must reframe from asking questions, conducting investigations, or even discussing the case with other scientists (jurors) until the very end of the procedure.[79]

Historical facts aside, I am more interested in pointing out that in addition to the fact that one may be hard pressed to substantively draw any distinction between fact and law, it is equally difficult to deny that the construction of fact is procedurally shaped by particular legal methods (theories) as well.

VI. Some Legal Implications

Once the fictitious distinction between fact and law, together with the segregation between fact and theory, as well as fact and value, are abandoned as epistemo-

---

[78] Coady, *Testimony: A Philosophical Study*, p. 62. An extensive discussion of issues of expert opinions concerning science, to which a flurry of commentary has appeared since the 1993 US Supreme Court *Daubert* decision, clearly is beyond the scope of this paper. For a highly readable treatment of the subject, see generally Kenneth R. Foster & Peter W. Huber, *Judging Science: Scientific Knowledge and the Federal Courts*, 1999.

[79] Larry Laudan, *Truth, Error, and Criminal Law: An Essay in Legal Epistemology*, 2006, pp. 216—217.

logically unfounded, many familiar dichotomies in law will require rethinking. The following issues are some of the more obvious examples of dualistic views that immediately become difficult to sustain.

1. Legal Syllogisms

If the application of law cannot possibly be the simple operation of syllogisms, one might ask what practical implications are for proving that the syllogistic operation is not actually a mode of legal reasoning? If the refutation makes no practical difference, then pragmatically there is no need to engage in the argument in the first place.[80]

I suggest, however, that by proving the operation of legal syllogisms unrealistic, lawyers can stop pretending that syllogisms are useful methods by which they can develop legal solutions with certainty. This general assertion further entails two implications: First, legal applications involve more than finding or using proper interpretative methods to law. Construction of facts should be equally important as, if not more so than, legal interpretations. Second, lawyers should not be overwhelmed by the sheer formalistic presentations of legal arguments in syllogisms. Although modern textbooks on logic sometimes also point out the unreliability of syllogisms as methods for legal reasoning, Francis Bacon actually mentioned the same point long ago that syllogisms, even as after thoughts for arranging arguments in the most compact forms, would be useful only insofar as all premises are free from ambiguities and errors.[81] To recognize the facts/law dichotomy as a myth in legal reasoning, lawyers must realize that legal solutions frequently require looking behind and beyond these formalistic arrangements of legal arguments by examining their background values and bias.

---

[80] William James, *Pragmatism: A New Name for an Old Way of Thinking*, Waking Lion Press, 2006, p. 22.

[81] Bacon, *The New Organon*, p. 35 ("The syllogism consists of propositions, propositions consist of words, and words are counters for notions. Hence if the notions themselves (this is the basis of the mater) are confused and abstracted from things without care, there is nothing sound in what is built on them.") This of course is not to suggest that challenges to the blind adherence to syllogisms have not been advanced since Bacon's date. For example, one of the most familiar controversies over usefulness of Hempel's deductive-nomological scientific explanation is the charge of the irrelevancy of the (basically deductive) method. *See* discussions in Curd & Cover, *Philosophy of Science: The Central Issues*, pp. 685—725, pp. 784—787.

2. The Fact/Law Dichotomy for the Jury and Judges

Although this is not a place for discussing the merits of the jury system, the collapse of the fact/law dichotomy makes it obvious that the involvement of the jury lies not so much in the inherent differences between fact and law as in a convention rooted in history and practical considerations.[82]

Regardless whether the methodology and epistemological outlook of the common law procedure historically have contributed to epistemological approaches in science, history and many other endeavors, Laudan wonders whether the shoe now is not on the other foot. Insofar as the determination of facts by the jury is concerned, he wrote:

> ...let us imagine telling scientists working on a problem...that they will be given access to only a subset of the available, relevant evidence. Further, they can put no questions to those feeding them relevant information. They cannot collect any evidence themselves, nor request its collection, nor consult any outside sources. Nor can they talk among themselves about the arguments pro and con until they have heard the full cases presented by their colleagues, and so on. No one would expect a system of inquiry constructed along such lines to be efficient, reliable, or long-lived.[83]

I suggest that so many rules for restricting deliberation by the jury are invented to try to confine jurors' role to what they are considered to be competent to evaluate, namely, the determination of fact, not of law. However, if the distinction between fact and law is an illusion, jurors' evaluation of fact can only be equivalent to (perhaps inchoate) construction of law.

3. Appellate Reviews of Law

Many civil law systems restrict appellate reviews to only the questions of law, not of fact. Under common law, facts as determined by the jury generally bind the court and would not be subject to review on appeals. The appellate courts usually defer to lower courts on issues of facts, insofar as the findings of facts are not clearly er-

---

[82] See Kim Lane Scheppele, *Facing Facts in Legal Interpretation: Questions of Law and Questions of Fact*, 30 Representatins 43 (1990).

[83] Laudan, *Truth, Error, and Criminal Law: An Essay in Legal Epistemology*, pp. 216—217.

roneous or do not constitute abuse of discretion.[84]

However, as it is said that facts and law are not easily separable, mixed questions of law and fact requiring the application of legal principles to historical fact usually receive a de novo review on appeals.[85] For example, whether or not there was probable cause to justify a warrantless search, whether a defendant had received the notice required by due process, was denied the effective assistance of counsel are questions of law for the appellate court without necessarily being "proved" as part of the adjudicative facts by the lower court. This has to be so simply because lawyers tried to hold on to the dichotomy of fact and law that in reality could not be drawn.

Because of the difficulties encountered in practice due to this artificial separation of fact and law, there are, at least under the U. S. law, signs indicating that appellate reviews are moving away from the rigid formalistic dichotomy of fact and law. For example, in criminal procedure, the sufficiency of evidence is reviewable.[86] It is obviously only a sheer legal fiction to continue to characterize sufficiency of evidence as "a question of law". Moreover, Antiterrorism and Effective Death Penalty Act of 1996, Section 2254, makes no definite distinction, in terms of deference, between questions of law and mixed questions of law and fact. Reviewable grounds consist of "unreasonable application of ... Federal law and unreasonable determination of the facts in light of the evidence presented in the State court proceeding".[87]

4. Adjudicative Facts and Legislative Facts

Since it is illusory to draw distinction between fact and law, adjudicative and "legislative facts" both contain legal theories. As a matter of fact, the US Federal Rules of Evidence states as much when it comes to "legislative facts". Since the

---

[84] In the US criminal procedure, appellate reviews have been traditionally divided into three different categories, namely, questions of law (de novo reviews), questions of facts (reviewable for clear error), and matters of abuse of discretion. Wayne R. Lafave, Jerold H. Israel, And Nancy J. King, *Criminal Procedure*, 4th ed., 2004, pp. 1296—1297. For difficulties encountered in the artificial distinction of legal issues from factual ones, see also Frederick Schauer, *Thinking Like a Lawyer: A New Introduction to Legal Reasoning*, 2009, pp. 212—218.

[85] Lafave, *Criminal Procedure*, p. 1298.

[86] It is said that the standard of appellate review of sufficiency of the evidence is meant to support a finding of guilt beyond a reasonable doubt. Stephen A. Saltzburg and Daniel J. Capra, *American Criminal Procedure: Cases and Commentary*, 7th ed., 2004, p. 1607.

[87] Ibid., At 1641. (Emphasis added).

court must take notice of "legislative facts" in the determination of adjudicative facts, the latter must be as theory-laden as, and cannot be distinguished from, the former.

While scholars like Schauer have recognized the serious implications that arise from this fictitious distinction between adjudicative and legislative "facts", they have not provided a solution to the problem.[88] I suggest that the difficulty actually has been created because lawyers invented and have continued to maintain the untenable distinction between these two "facts" (and theories of course). Once the basic dichotomy between them, just as that between fact and law, is discarded, the logical conclusion seems to dictate that legislative "facts" should either be proved just like adjudicative facts, or at least they must be clearly articulated in court's decisions and be subject to challenge on appeals or during the arguments.

5. Concrete and Abstract Reviews

Scholars sometimes distinguish abstract from concrete reviews at the appellate level. For example, in most of the centralized constitutional review systems, such as the German Constitutional Court, it is said that the Court review only legal issues in abstract, as distinguished from concrete reviews involving facts of specific cases.

Abandonment of the fact/law dichotomy makes the distinction between concrete and abstract reviews highly suspicious in the sense that the distinction may be for the convenience of the discussion, but it lacks real merits in substance. For one thing, most of the so-called abstract reviews of law are triggered by disputes or doubts arising from specific cases. To characterize the appellate reviews as abstract is to say that the Court will pretend that it will not pay attention to the underlying factual background calling for the interpretation. Nor will the Court attend to the practical consequences of the interpretation since it concerns itself only with the abstract analysis of the law. To the extent this artificial distinction could be made (and I have already made it clear that it could not), the review of legal issues and the abstract interpretation of law would almost be a bad ones. For another thing, as fact and law could not possibly so separated, the so-called abstract reviews of only law are largely a fiction. To say the least, abstract reviews will by necessity also review doctrinal

---

[88] Schauer, *Thinking Like a Lawyer: A New Introduction to Legal Reasoning*, p. 216, n. 34.

and historical facts which may or may not made obvious in the reviewed disputes.

Another reason for rejecting such artificial distinction of abstract and concrete reviews lies in the fact that abstraction and concreteness are two extremes of something like a continuum. Therefore, they are relative concepts instead of two complete separate categories. As such, B which is abstract as compared with C, may nevertheless be very concrete as compared with A. We simply do not have objective standards by which we can say for certainty that something definite is abstract. The distinction, therefore, is only a convention in scholars' parlance, and a bad one at that.

VII. Conclusions

Traditionally, lawyers believe that fact and law belong to two different categories, and that they are inherently different, even though they may overlap from time to time. I have proposed that such a distinction, just like the dichotomy between fact and theory, as well as fact and value, is not tenable.

In addition to the fusion of fact and law, I pointed out that legal procedure provides numerous rules and methods for the determination of reliable facts. These rules and methods historically influenced the construction of scientific facts in natural sciences and are the foundation for the determination of legal facts. In other words, legal facts not only are inseparable from legal theories in a substantive way, they are procedurally determined by legal theories (rules and methods) as well.

To discard the erroneous dichotomy between fact and law requires lawyers to rethink the adequacy of certain legal categories and classifications. These archaic dualisms include the realization that the solution to legal problems is far from a simple application of law using proper interpretation to facts. They are from the very beginning the construction of legal theories. Under this basic view, some familiar dichotomies such as fact/law division respectively for the jury and judges, reviews of issues of law as distinguishable from those of facts, the distinction between adjudicative and legislative "facts", as well as abstract and concrete reviews all become unsustainable.

The Concept of Governmentality in Michel Foucault as His Last Negation of Law

João Chaves

I. Introduction

In the last decade, the number of papers and researches from legal scholars and theorists on the works of the French philosopher Michel Foucault (1926—1984) has grown. Most of these approaches are concerned with the search for Foucaldian answers to substantial juridical questions, as the problem of power of punitive systems, although attempts to identify, in the author's work, critical thought able to renew the present legal theory are also common.

There is a certain degree of optimism amongst legal scholars when dealing with issues originally proposed by Foucault—at least in Brazilian scene. When one classifies him as "the philosopher of madness" or suggests that the work he developed is all based on the proposition that "power is everywhere", one generates the conviction that there is a Foucaldian solution to some problems of legal studies. That means the Foucaldian thought could originate a new array of alternatives for the understanding of this social phenomenon in a post-modernist context, in which the legal discourse loses its traditional basis and seeks foundation in new standards of rationality. Nevertheless, such a critical approach is not easily observed over Foucault himself, specially about his frankly underestimated and, as we will see, negative view of Law.

In this context, the aim of this paper is to outline, in a satisfactory way, the most significative images of Law in works of Michel Foucault, beginning with his archeological period, which started with the book *Madness and Civilization* (*L'histoire de la folie à l'âge classique*) and went on from the early 1960's until the end of 1970's, and finishing with the courses *Security, Territory, Population* (*Sécurité, territoire, population*) and *The Birth of Biopolitics* (*Naissance de la biopolitique*), to conclude, finally, with comments on the real importance the French author attributed to the legal thinking.

The danger of erroneous and non-systematic interpretations of Foucaldian isolated concepts—that is, the ones that ignore its internal coherence and historicity—justifies this task and is the starting point for a methodological option. For this reason, my research is concentrated in an internal reading of Foucault's books, courses and essays, with the support of Brazilian and international literature on the subject, and does not have any connection with legal theory—at least in its traditional form. My initial and basic hypothesis is that Foucault, as a non-legal thinker, takes the legal problems only in a casuistic way amongst others issues that he judges more relevant, which leads to the conclusion that it is impossible to identify a "Foucaldian legal theory". The extension of this suggestion to its last consequences will produce the main conclusion of this essay: in various moments and specially with the concept of governmentality created in 1978, Michel Foucault implicitly puts forward or suggests the denial of Law as a discursive framework, which would eliminate all attempts of creating specific and autonomous legal theories.

II. First Negation: Law in Michel Foucault's Works between 1963 and 1975

First of all, I would like to deal with the initial period of Foucault's work, generally classified as the archeological period. It is possible to perceive early on reference to law by the author.

The image of Law to be first explored in *Madness and Civilization* is not related to the modern reforms of psychiatry, as would be easier to conclude. It is more adequately included in a wide-scale conclusion: the experience of madness in the Classical Age contains both medical and correctional aspects.

In fact, Foucault wants to show that in a specific historical moment (the Classical Age) the judge was forced to make use of a medical diagnosis in order to recognize cases of madness, even when it would be possible to identify the insane without any further formality (as in the case of those who cannot even express their will). Foucault concludes that the connection between judges and physicians to state madness in trials was not an incidental support or technical help to the legal knowledge. It would be better understood as a dislocation of decisory spheres, so that physicians, and not judges, were competent to examine and find out the truth regarding these individuals.

An example of it can be useful. In a conflict of two documents in a trial—a judge decision and a medical diagnosis—registered in 17th Century, the philosopher points out two knowledge levels, that break up the legal context and the medical isolation:

> In one case, it [the medicine] questions the capacity of legal subject, then prepares a psychology which will mix, in some hesitant unity, an analysis of mental abilities and a legal analysis of the capacity of make contracts and oblige himself. It aims the very structures of civil liberties. In the other, it remarks the conducts of social men and prepares a dualistic pathology in terms of normal and abnormal, healthy and sick, dividing in two irreducible camps the simple formula: "ready to confine".[1]

On one hand, that is not a specific reflexion on Law, but only an allusion to an alleged "legal theory" whose long experience of classification would be recycled by the positivist psychiatric science of the 19th century. However, in no moment does Foucault identify more details on what the theoretical legacy from the concept of legal subjectivity would be, there referred as a decaying construction which goes in the Modern Age in symbiosis with the medical discourse. On the other hand, the reading

---

[1] Michel Foucault, *Histoire de la folie à l'âge classique*, Paris: Gallimard, 1972, p. 174.

of *Madness and Civilization* further supports the idea that Law is just a mask for other discursive practices, maybe more recent and suitable for the modern needs of the present mechanisms of power/knowledge.

In *Truth and Juridical Forms* (*A verdade e as formas jurídicas*), a course given in Brazil in 1973, Foucault promotes a great twist on the classical readings of Sophocles' *Oedipus the King*. Following the same path of Deleuze and Guattari's studies, he does not exactly see the incestuous conflict, but the description of truth-making proceedings—some of them with prophetical, and others with judicial character. Foucault wants to demonstrate that Sophocles' tragedy is in fact a kind of police thriller, in which a main character wishes to rebuild a historical truth, assuming the right to produce truth by witnesses rather than oraculous prophecies. The original turn in this and other tragedies was, in Foucault's point of view, the beginning of a new regime of truth, with evidence as the main juridical form—the first birth of judicial inquiry.[2]

Through the study of inquiry, which would be recovered after a long period of obscurity in the scientific *episteme*, Foucault traces the genealogy of a juridical structure, in fact the structure that exists in our present in terms of truth production, but continues not to discuss directly about the legal field.

Again we see in a Foucaldian work the Law described as cover for a new power/knowledge arrangement (knowledge practices associated with power relations), in a space of legitimation completely strange to itself. Beyond of this, there is also the admission of a Nietzschean vision about truth applied to Law, a search of the violent and secret origins of the truth production. This genealogy of modern Law would produce, as Foucault supposes, a turning point to the real struggles of its constitution and the birth of the subjects that compose the legal field.[3] With this conclusion, I can develop the idea of an opposition in Foucault between what D'Alessandro called

---

[2] Michel Foucault, *A verdade e as formas jurídicas*, Rio de Janeiro: Nau, 2002, pp. 54—63.

[3] Michel Foucault, "Nietzsche, la généalogie, l'histoire", in *Dits et Écrits*, v. 1, n. 84, Paris: Gallimard, 2001, p. 1008; Lucio D'Alessandro, "La verité et les formes juridiques", in *Michel Foucault: trajectoires au coeur du présent*, ed. Lucio D'Alessandro and Adolfo Marino, Paris: L'Harmattan, 1998, p. 137.

"*normative kantism of legal culture*"[4] and his beloved model of justice as a war ritual.

Truth and Juridical Forms, in the same way as *Abnormal* (*Les anormaux*), a course from the early months of 1975, are part of the genealogical period of Foucaldian thought, in which the mechanisms of power/knowledge take place as the basic theme. At this time the classical book *Discipline and Punish* (*Surveiller et punir*) is published. Through the description of an emerging disciplinary power and the use of examples such as the growth of prison/penitentiary social structures, it puts forth once more a weak version of Law.

When Foucault explains the replacement of suplice by other forms of punishment, special attention is given to the notion of crime. He emphasizes that the judicial institutions do not judge individual conducts of criminals—the so called "judicial objects defined by the Code"[5]. The main point is the incompatibilities of the subjects and the means exposed, like their passions and abnormalities. This was written by him in order to avoid misunderstandings of the legal theory, a way of escaping those who would see the social judgement as a secondary effect of crime punishments. It is an actual evaluation, but always auxiliary.

I would think this is a deeply negative image of Law. After all, Foucault does not deny its existence as a part of the punitive processes, but imposes to the Law the role of mere justification, because the real judgement is "normalized" rather than legal-normative. In a brief synthesis, "today's judge does something else but not 'judge'"[6].

Michel Foucault's success with the recasting of the debate on Law and its importance nowadays comes from a specific answer that could be presented against him. Thus, if norms and statutes are a fantasy from sovereign authority and, in our post-Enlightenment society, the disciplinary mechanisms of control are oversized and take all the space, would it be possible to imagine that Law in our times is transmitted by

---

[4] Lucio D'Alessandro, "La verité et les formes juridiques", *op. cit.*, 138. In the same path of the opposition of Kant and Foucault, Pierre Macherey sees the problem of an immanence (and non-trancendence) about norm and action in Foucault, as in Spinoza. Pierre Macherey, "Pour une histoire naturelle des normes", in *Michel Foucault Philosophe—Rencontre Internationale*, ed. various authors Paris: Seuil, 1989, pp. 212—217.

[5] Michel Foucault, *Surveiller et punir*, Paris: Gallimard, 1975, p. 25.

[6] Ibid., pp. 27—28.

disciplinary—and non-juridical—forms?

The answer to this question reveals a relevant theoretical consideration if we want to establish an image of Law in *Discipline and Punish*. That happens because Foucault does not see a connexion between Law and discipline, which are in no moment related to each other by any means. The image created is similar to a parallelism: the author repeats that the *contract* is the ideal form of Law, while *panopticon* becomes the technique of disciplines; the panoptical power on its turn is not submitted to juridical-political power, being in fact absolutely independent from it. The disciplines form the underground of civil liberties, a dark side with its own development.

Foucault even contemplates the existence of a subordination of the disciplinary to the juridical, when the discipline was an "underlaw", which extends the political action to the level of singularities not directly comprehended by the sovereignty discourse. Meanwhile, the author himself refuses this version and defends the opposite one: discipline is a kind of "outlaw", the inside out of an extreme division.

If we take the general image of Law in *Discipline and Punish*, here summarized, an obvious principle is therefore perceived: in this work of Foucault there is neither a theoretical object called "Law" nor the tiniest interest in studying it, in a movement considered by Hunt and Wickam as an expulsion of Law from Modernity.[7] It is, as previously mentioned, a minor theme, in spite of traditional voices on the subject. As it remains, we can only conceive perspectives of future developments and answers for apories left aside, although some critics doubt the workability of a project like that. However, there is a strong negation: now Law loses its advantage in the normative order of society, and is challenged by the exotic dissociation between Law and juridical forms. Are we experiencing a weak "law" from new mechanisms like disciplines, which is free of the classical Law?

---

[7] Alan Hunt and Gary Wickham, *Foucault and Law: Towards a Sociology of Law as Governance*, Chicago: Pluto Press, 1994, pp. 46—49.

III. Second Negation: the Law at *Society Must Be Defended* (1976)

Society Must Be Defended (*Il faut défendre la société*) is a course given at *Collège de France* in the beginning of 1976. This chronological note is important: after all, the classes were a result of the first research of Michel Foucault after the course *Abnormal* in 1975 and the publication of the book *Discipline and Punish* at the same year. As a moment of pause and new reflections after a hard work on the constitution of the discipline mechanism and new power/knowledge dynamics, the course was entirely devoted to a commentary about the uprising of a "historical discourse from perspective", a kind of genealogy of modern history.

Moreover, Foucault proceeds to the genealogy of modern States to observe that, in fact, they are not based on the well-known thesis of sovereign and original legitimity. The author reveals that the period of liberal revolutions backed a "race discourse", the creation of a new national body to justify violence against all internal and external enemies. The lightening idea of a revolutionary emancipation is swapped, at least in Foucault's thought, by the suggestion of a "racism of State", the inclusion of the permanent war as a criterion of political operation.[8]

It is in this course, meanwhile, that we can perceive a more specific attention to the legal question. Foucault chooses the legal theorists as possible debaters in his genealogical perspective. What he calls "classical legal theory", in which the political power is granted by an authentic legal act, is again replaced by the "rule of War" as the standard for power relations. Because of this he refuses the economical analysis of relations as unfair exchanges, because "economicism" is connected to the legal notion of power.

There is one more incisive provocation. To the author, Law is merely an internal historiography of State, a knowledge useful only to salute the monarchy and blind to anything outside itself, blind even to the social forces. He tends, therefore, to ignore Law because of its inability to go beyond the official truth or to denounce the ge-

---

[8] Michel Foucault, "*Il faut défendre la société*"—*Cours au Collège de France, 1976*, Paris: Seuil, Gallimard, 1997, pp. 37—41.

nealogy of the truth regime where it is inserted.[9]

Foucault, once again, explains that the figure of the central and sovereign power cease to exist, but is slowly invaded by plenty of different practices of biological control on individuals. In this context, Law does not disappear, but is in fact penetrated by another form of Law, based on a reversal power, which is close to the the relational and non-economic power idea of the disciplinary mechanism and far from the traditional political power concept. This "new Law" comprises sovereignty, but overlaps it by a strategy of original spread controls and a different power/knowledge regime. To Foucault, the legal theory rapidly perceived this transition, but because of its inability to abandon the essentialist notion of Law as a complex of relations among autonomous subjects, could not develop beyond the repetition of that same history of universalization—which was already emphasized all throughout the course *Society Must Be Defended*.[10] The author concludes of the inadequacy of all the recent legal theory, at least in its most common versions.

More than a mask of real dominations by a game of symbolic representations, Law is, in Foucault's words, an appendix of the centralized and repressive model of power, which is strongly criticized throughout the genealogical period. While the sovereignty mechanism gives liberties within limits, discipline as a global mechanism produces the normalization (and not the old "normativism") of all human acts by strict policies. As a consequence, sovereignty becomes a mask of disciplinary power after the 17th Century, since the old monarchies until modern day parliamentary democracies, which, in his opinion, are only alternative practices to the same old—and old-fashioned—diagram.[11] Just as in *Discipline and Punish*, Foucault confirms the radical break-up of Law from disciplines, as of the juridical-normative dimension and the social normalization processes.

The response for this gap is indicated by Foucault with the proposal of a "new form of right" (*nouveau droit*), thus described: "It is not through recourse to sovereignty against discipline that the effects of disciplinary power can be limited, because sovereignty and disciplinary mechanisms are two absolutely integral constituents in

---

[9] Ibid., p. 155.
[10] Ibid., p. 214.
[11] Ibid., p. 30.

the general mechanism of power in our society. If one wants to look for a nondisciplinary form of power, or rather, to struggle against disciplines and disciplinary power, it is not towards the ancient right of sovereignty that one should turn, but towards the possibility of a new form of right, one which must indeed be antidisciplinarian, but at the same time liberated from the principle of sovereignty."[12]

This proposal of a new form of right (or new Law, as a traduction of *nouveau droit*) was however not brought up by Michel Foucault in later works.[13] Nevertheless, some researches had been developed on this subject, with both optimist and negative conclusions—and, in my point of view, often useless for any other purpose.

I would prefer to work not with its possible core or internal secret content, but rather identify, in its conception, two internal characteristics of the Foucaldian way of thinking.

The first of them is what I would like to call the *paradox of the expected resistance*. As Foucault said, there is no exit for the power nets. If our author has formulated an intelligent and prior answer to critics, and that is the mutual connection of power and resistance as opposite forces in the mechanisms, he asserts that this very mechanism has no escape exit. In other words, power and resistance are different but as they are put together in the same complex, they become linked and not dissociable in a critical analysis, in a sort of mutual nourishing.

This conclusion can be easily inferred from one of the possible readings of Foucault's work, which would describe a long and wide-ranging space of norm without an exterior and would cover both what is compatible and what is different, or even abnormal to itself.[14] If everything is inside the homogeneous space of thought in interdependence, everything is equal and nothing beyond that (the different) is possible anymore. In a simple way, any Other would be, if well observed, just the other side of the Equal, as a negative reflex of this.

---

[12] Ibid., p. 35.

[13] Márcio Fonseca, *Michel Foucault e o direito*, São Paulo: Max Limonad, 2002, p. 242; Carole Smith, "The sovereign state v. Foucault: law and disciplinary power", in *The Sociological Review*, v. 48, n. 2, 2000, p. 298; Roger Mourad, "After Foucault—a new form of right", in *Philosophy & Social Criticism*, v. 29, n. 4, 2003, p. 456; Brent Pickett, "Foucaultian rights?", in *The Social Science Journal*, v. 37, n. 3, 2000, p. 404.

[14] François Ewald, "Un pouvoir sans dehors", in *Michel Foucault Philosophe—Rencontre Internationale*, ed. various authors, Paris: Seuil, 1989, p. 200.

The second great characteristic is the frequent Foucaldian *appeal to the Outside* as an impossible dimension of discursive constitution. This Outside is not the margin, but something more difficult to observe. It is close to an alternative dimension against power/knowledge, an unidentified place without pertinence to our plan of reality. For Deleuze [15], this Outside in Foucault and also in Blanchot and Bataille is the unshaped element of forces, which comes from it and in it traces their relations. An Outside as a part of the real space constituted just by virtualities. I can guess that, to escape from the paradox of the expected resistance, Foucault needed to create at least one chance to escape from the diagrams of power/knowledge. This last conclusion justifies this appeal to the Outside in Foucault as the place for new practice constitutions and new resistances against the mechanisms. Despite that, this appeal is better described as a literary figure rather than a positive social construction.

In a recent work I have also concluded that these two points—the search for a paradoxal resistance and an utopist Outside—are the genesis of the debility of the "new form of right" concept from *Society Must Be Defended*.[16] There would not be any possible development on that way, because its circular and autophagical conception leads to a strong presumption that there is also no exit to the rise of a new Law alongside both sovereignty and disciplinary mechanisms. That opens, for me, the second implicit negation: Foucault works with the image of a "sovereign Law" as a fact of the past that exists today rooted only in custom (and in the beliefs and dreams of legal theorists), and, at the same time, does not allow any revival on the juridical field, here designed as a route to other—and frankly non-juridical—mechanisms of power/knowledge.

IV. Third and Last Negation: Governmentality *vs.* Law

After dismissal and denial of the presumptions adopted by the traditional legal theory, Michel Foucault once again mentions the problem of Law between 1978 and 1979, in the courses *Security, Territory, Population* and *The Birth of Biopolitics*.

---

[15] Gilles Deleuze, *Foucault*, Paris: Minuit, 1986, pp. 128—130.
[16] João Chaves, *O problema do direito novo em Michel Foucault: entre a resistência e o Fora*. LL. M. diss. (Federal University of Pernambuco, 2006).

In the first course, the study of biopower starts by the admission of the new mechanism of security, different from both sovereignty and discipline. Foucault's genealogy is clear in its purposes: an indication of how, from a certain point of time, there has emerged a new art of government as a result of the generalization of Christian pastoral techniques and the beginning of the "governmental reason" in the modern States. In this moment, the new practice or mechanism of governmentality arises.

In *The Birth of Biopolitics*, Foucault links the appearance of intensive biological control of populations with neoliberalism, here considered as a new form of modulation of the struggle of governors and the governed. He tries to show that, in the middle of the 18th Century, governmentality hands to the market structures the top position as the place of truth production.

Returning once again to *Security, Territory, Population*, the Law is mentioned in the first lessons, when Foucault discusses the birth of the security mechanism after the consolidation of disciplinary and the weakening of sovereignty mechanisms. The referral to Law appears when the author foresees criticism regarding the excess of mechanisms in a casual and non-logic succession. He defends that there is no line with isolated stages—to him, "there is no the legal era, disciplinary era or security era"[17]—but rather a mix of various mechanisms, and this mix is always transforming itself.

For the first time there is an explicit distinction between Law and discipline, which, with the new mechanism of security, would compose a trio of enchained mechanisms present with the help of legal forms, always used as diffusion tactics. The Law, to Foucault, is the bright dominium that forbids disorder. Discipline, as an opposite, carries an intensive power: it only allows what is authorized in advance. Between the two above, remains security, as a control by permanent regulation both on forbidding and inciting until the limitation of the material reality.

In his words, Law is a form of thinking order from disorder, by restrictions:

> It is by the point of view of disorder, in a progressive analysis, that we can establish the order. The order, that is what remains after we forbid eve-

---

[17] Michel Foucault, *Sécurité, territoire, population—Cours au Collège de France, 1977—1978*, Paris: Seuil, Gallimard, 2004, p. 10.

rything that now composes the interdicted. It is this negative thinking that, in my opinion, is the characteristic of a legal code. Negative thinking and techniques.[18]

As a comparison, we can see the Foucault's synthesis for discipline and security mechanisms (and its differences):

The discipline, in its very definition, rules everything. The discipline does not leave anything outside it—nothing can escape from it. The principle of discipline is that even the small facts cannot be abandoned by itselves. The smallest infraction to discipline must be observed with attention, as small as it is. The mechanism of security, by other side, allows the actions of individuals (laisse faire). It is not question of allow everything, but create some levels where the action is necessary.[19]

If, in *Discipline and Punish* as the course *Society Must Be Defended*, Foucault admits that the legal discourse of sovereignty is incompatible with discipline, being more a remainder than an actual part of our present diagram, in this *Security, Territory, Population* both Law and sovereignty are included in a complex game of mediations of ancient and new mechanisms of power/knowledge. Then, where should the Law's anachronism stay? Can we conclude that, in Foucault's late 1970's thought, the legal forms subsist, although debarred of the judicial model of power, and are now pieces of a non-legal governmentality? In this point of view, I would agree that Foucault banishes the old Law from our Modern times and offers the idea of postmodernist legal theory as the theory of the government arts.

With *The Birth of Biopolitics*, Foucault continues his revision of early images, and now can connect governmentality and Law in the same settling in a satisfactory mode. In the Middle Age Law was an intensifying agent of the monarchic power against feudal power. From late 18th Century it will appear as an exterior limit which, by the classic way of statutes and judicial institutions as courts, moderates the practices of governmentality.[20] In many moments Foucault mentions what he calls a "legal inflation", but not to conclude that Law is, as in the past, the main strategical

---

[18] Ibid., p.47.
[19] Ibid., pp.46—47.
[20] Ibid., p.9.

space for truth production. In this new version of his thought, Law stop figuring as an organic part of sovereign discourse to be reborn as technique of mediation of individuals and State in the same 'economic game.[21]

V. Conclusions

From a leading role to a simple remainder of a medieval mechanism, the Law in Foucault's works loses its own theorical dimension and grows into one of the small strategies of the new mechanism of modern governmentality. We may call it expulsion, disappearance, weakness or just the end of a way of thinking—as Foucault declared in a more romantic form with the man as a face on the sand, at *The Order of Things*.[22] In all this possibilities, there is a common point: Foucault does not see Law as we see, because of the small importance given by him to our studies and abstract construction. In despite of this, the Foucaldian approach in its many moments and internal transitions leaves us a question: does a "proper of Law", on which its theorists could concentrate all of their efforts not exist anymore? In all his negations, specially in the third and last one, Michel Foucault provokes and defies all of us, as legal theorists, to think one again about the role of our legal theory in these postmodernist days and also question if Law even exists—and if we still have to really care about it.

---

[21] Ibid., p.169.
[22] Michel Foucault, *Les mots et les choses*, Paris: Gallimard, 1966, p.398.

本辑作者名录
List of the Authors

1. 奥弗·拉班,美国俄勒冈大学法学院副教授,博士,美国俄勒冈州尤金市玛瑙大街1515号
   Ofer Raban, Associate Professor, Dr., University of Oregon School of Law, 1515 Agate Street, Eugene Oregon, USA

2. 迪亚哥·普尔,西班牙胡安卡洛斯国王大学,马德里图利潘大街,28933,莫斯托莱斯校区
   Diego Poole, Universidad Rey Juan Carlos—Calle Tulipán s/n. 28933 Móstoles. Madrid, Spain

3. 努诺·科尔霍,巴西圣保罗大学副教授
   Nuno M. M. S. Coelho, Associate Professor of University of Sao Paulo, Brazil

4. 汉讷·伊索拉-米提伦,芬兰国家审计办公室高级审计员,行政科学硕士
   Hannele Isola-Miettinen, Licentiate of Administrative Sciences, Senior Auditor, National Audit Office, Finland

5. 马里扬·帕夫克比克,哲学博士,斯洛文尼亚卢布尔雅那大学法律理论和法律社会学教授
   Marijan Pavčnik, PhD, Chair for Legal Theory and Sociology of Law, University of Ljubljana, Slovenia

6. 弗里德里希·拉赫梅尔,奥地利维也纳因斯布鲁克大学教授
   Friedrich Lachmayer, Professor, University of Innsbruck, Vienna, Austria

7. 阿尔贝特·维斯帕兹阿尼,意大利莫利塞大学社会科学和行政法副教授
   Alberto Vespaziani, Associate Professor, University of Molise, Italy

8. 埃伊莱姆·尤米特·艾迪甘,土耳其安卡拉大学法学院副教授,土耳其安卡

拉市,杰贝吉校区
Eylem Ümit Atilgan, Associate Professor, Law Faculty, Ankara University, Cebeci, Ankara, Turkey

9. 张嘉尹,台湾世新大学法学系专任副教授,台北市木栅路一段17巷1号
Chia-yin Chang, Associate Professor, Shih Hsin University, 1 Lane17 Sec. 1, Mu-Cha Rd. Taipei, Taiwan, R. O. C

10. 黄维幸,台湾世新大学法学系客座教授,台北市木栅路一段17巷1号
Thomas Weishing Huang, Professor of Law, Shih Hsin University, 1 Lane17 Sec. 1, Mu-Cha Rd. Taipei, Taiwan, R. O. C

11. 霍奥·查维斯,巴西伯南布哥联邦大学法律硕士,伯南布哥天主教大学副教授
João Chaves, LL. M. at Federal University of Pernambuco (Brazil); Assistant Professor at Catholic University of Pernambuco (Brazil)

引 证 体 例
Citation Rules

一、引证的基本规则

1. 引证以必要为限。
2. 引证应是已发表之文献。引证未发表文献应征得相关权利人之同意。
3. 引证应保持被引证话语之原貌。
4. 引证应以注释准确地显示被引证作品之相关信息。

二、引证体例示例

1. 著作引文注释

（1）专著或编辑作品

作者著/编:《书名》（卷或册），出版社出版年，页码。（括注部分可省）

① 郑永流:《法治四章》，中国政法大学出版社2002年版，第369页。

② 梁治平编:《法律的文化解释》，生活·读书·新知三联书店1994年版，第36页。

③ Ronald Dworkin, *Taking Rights Seriously*, Harvard University Press, 1977, pp. 6—7.

④ Ronald L. Cohen (ed.), *Justice: Views from the Social Sciences*, Plenum Press, 1986, p. 31.

(2) 译著

〔国别〕作者:《书名或文章名》(卷或册),译者,出版社出版年,页码。

① 〔法〕孟德斯鸠:《论法的精神》(上册),张雁深译,商务印书馆1961年版,第91页。

2. 文章引文注释

(1) 期刊/报纸中的文章

作者:《文章名》,载《书名或杂志名》年代和期数。

① 张千帆:《从管制到自由》,载《北大法律评论》(第6卷第2辑),北京大学出版社2005年版。

② 贺卫方:《"契约"与"合同"的辨析》,载《法学研究》1992年第2期。

③ 贾林男:《银商与中国银联商号之争》,载《中华工商时报》2007年5月23日。

④ Robert J. Steinfeld, " Property and Suffrage in the Early American Republic", 41 *Stanford Law Review* 335 (1989).

(2) 编辑作品中的文章

作者:《文章名》,载编辑作品主编人:《编辑作品名称》,出版社出版年,页码。

① 陈弘毅:《从福柯的〈规训与惩罚〉看后现代思潮》,载朱景文主编:《当代西方后现代法学》,法律出版社2002年版,第223页。

② H. L. A. Hart, "Positivism and the Separation of Law and Morals", in H. L. A. Hart (ed.), *Essays in Jurisprudence and Philosophy*, Clarendon Press, 1983, pp. 57—58.

3. 网络资源注释

作者:《文章名》,网址,最后访问时间。

① 朱苏力:《司法制度的变迁》,http://law-thinker.com/show.asp?id=2926,最后访问于2005年11月9日。

② The Council of Australia Governments, *Water Reform Framework*, available at http://www.disr.gov.au/science/pmsec/14meet/inwater/app3form.html, last visited 21/07/2003.